# INTRODUCTION

This project started in 2005 when Ben Jakobsen sent me resin copies of the masters he made for the Jaguar Elefant interior. In 2013 I decided to start building the kit but I couldn't find good reference and the reference available showed that the kit interior wasn't correct. Lack of reference is the reason why Ben couldn't make a completely accurate interior and this was going to be the same problem for me too. Some way into the project I received help from Johannes Schneider and Per Sonnervik. They kindly shared information and reference to help me to slowly continue this build. Per sent an email to the curator of the U.S. Army Ordnance Museum to ask if they could provide us with some photos taken during the restoration of Fgst.Nr. 150071, if possible interior photos. To our surprise we received some photos within a few weeks, and even more to our surprise we were asked what else we needed. For months curators Gregory Hagge and Tina Desmoralis spent hours inside Fgst.Nr. 150071 to photograph everything we asked for and more! They even removed the sloping floor and the cover beneath it to show us the e-motors. Suddenly I had all the material I needed to complete this project. With the reference I now had I decided not to build just an Elefant interior, but to build Fgst.Nr 150071 with Nr. 102 on it's sides when captured by US troops in 1944.

This book shows the construction of my model and also some of the reference I used. Sadly the interior of Fgst.Nr.150071 is in a

very poor condition. Much of the thinner metal is gone due to corrosion, but remarkably there is still interior paint and even stencilling present. The new material together with some pictures of the Kubinka Ferdinand, wartime photographs (factory and wrecks), and the D-656 manuals enabled me to complete this interior build. You will see that despite being a large vehicle the interior space is limited for the crew. It also must have been noisy and hot with all engines and fans running, and maintenance would have been difficult because acces to engines, generators and e-motors is limited.

The kit I used as the basis for this build is the Dragon Sdkfz. 184 Elefant (6126). The entire interior is scratchbuild except for the two Maybach engines, using styrene sheet, tube and rod, copper and lead wire, and some brass sheet. The two Maybach HL120 TRM engines are from CMK, Aber photoetched details and Friul tracks are the only aftermarket items used. Many of the utilised Dragon kit parts also needed corrections. The model is build in sub-assemblies and these remain removable like the real thing, except for the removable fighting compartment roof panel

Hopefully this book will be an aid for those who want to build their own Ferdinand/Elefant interior and of interest for those who are interested in this vehicle or German armour in general.

# ①

# HULL

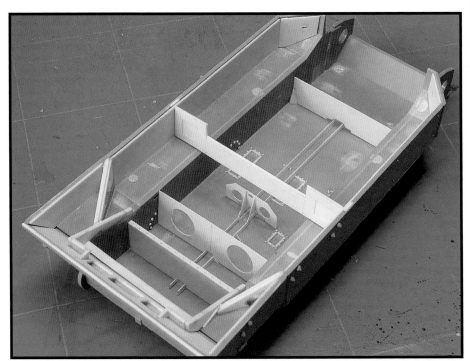

**Left** With styrene the hull armour is increased to scale thickness. Also the extended corners on the angled rear sides, originally the VK.4501(P), are added as are the dividing walls and other hull detail. The circular positioned bolt heads are for the suspension swing arm axles.

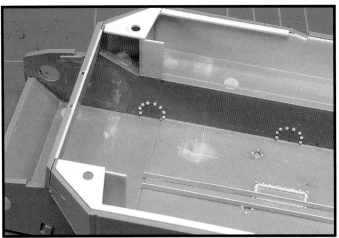

The drivers frontal armour thickened and compartment side walls added

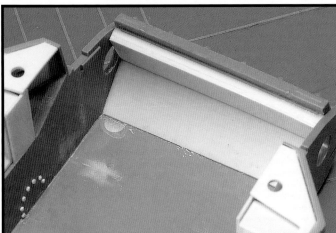

The three frontal armour plates increased to scale thickness.

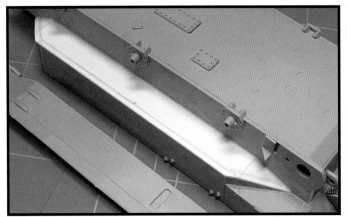

With the kit fenders going to be replaced by Aber PE ones the sponson undersides are made thicker to replace this part of the kit fender, and welds are added.

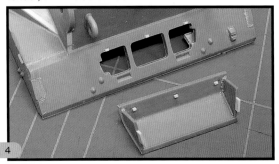

The gun platform and the 'Brücke' (Bridge). Two parts on to which the gun carriage will be mounted.

**Left** The armoured vent cover received some detail. Later I found out that the vent openings needed some dimensional correction.

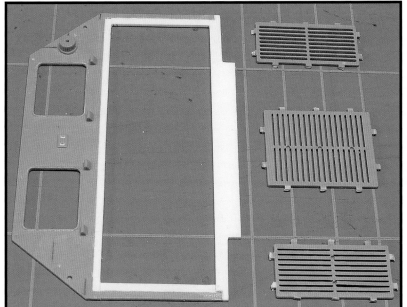

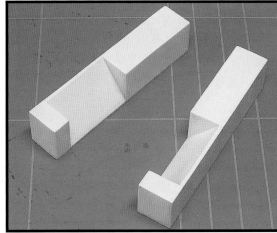

**Left** To determine fuel tank and radiator dimensions the Ferdinand louvers are cut from the deck plate and corrections are made.

**Above** The basic shapes of the fuel tanks. Factory photos show some hulls received a shorter tank on the rhs.

This photo shows why I needed the deck to be corrected. It made it possible to determine width of the radiators, the recess in the fuel tanks and position of the firewall.

The two Maybach engines with generators test fitted. The engines are from CMK.

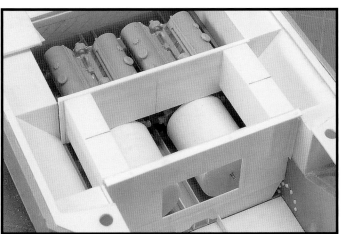

With the deck removed it's visible how the cooling unit sits inside the vehicle. Fit of things is so tight that lots of test fitting and correcting was needed to make things fit correctly.

**Right** Six fan shrouds, four for the radiators, two for the fans in the rear of the vehicle. All with eighteen vanes.

**Right** Four eight bladed fans were constructed for the radiator cooling fans.

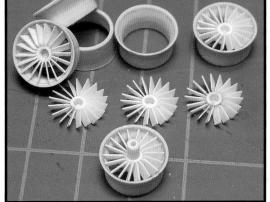

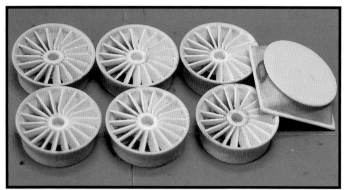

**Left** The base of the shroud (on the right) is a master and used to cast four identical pieces.

**Right** The completed shrouding. The vanes still need to be thinned and bolt detail will be added later.

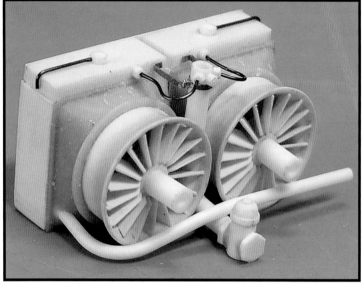

The Right Hand radiator/fan assembly. The Left Hand is mirrored to this one.

The outer side also will receive more detail later.

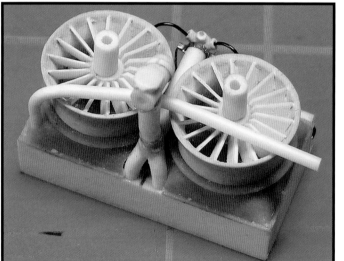

On the two outer corners hot water enters the radiators, the rear pipe on the lower right corner still needs to be added. The centre pipes return cooled water to the engines (oil coolers) on top is a valve to close the cooling circuit during cold starts or coolant exchange with another vehicle (Kuhlwasserübertragung).

**Above right** The drives that transfer power from the engines to the fans.

**Right** To align the drives with the radiators correctly a jig is made with the dimensions of the available space.

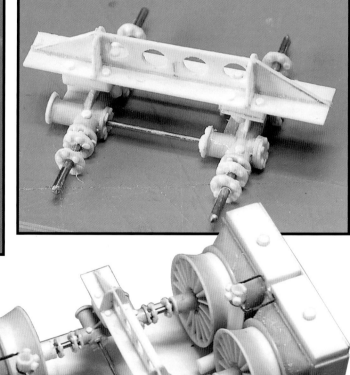

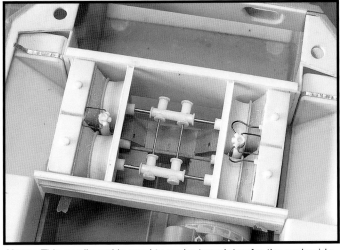

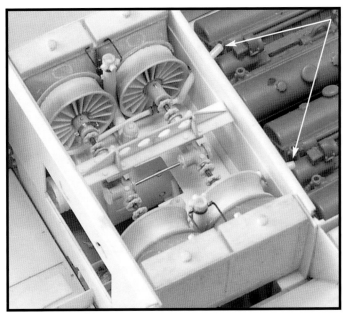

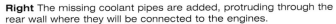

**Above** Thin cardboard is used to make templates for the underside of the cooling unit.

**Right** The missing coolant pipes are added, protruding through the rear wall where they will be connected to the engines.

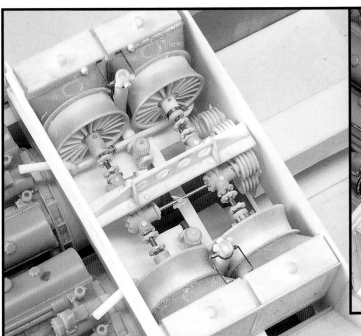

**Above left** The drive belt wheels are made from two different diameter disks glued together.

**Above** The completed cooling unit, except for the hand wheels on the valves. The rear coolant lines meet the engines at the brass manifolds. Deep inside the cooling unit the flexible return lines are visible.

**Right** Just like in reality, the cooling unit is removable.

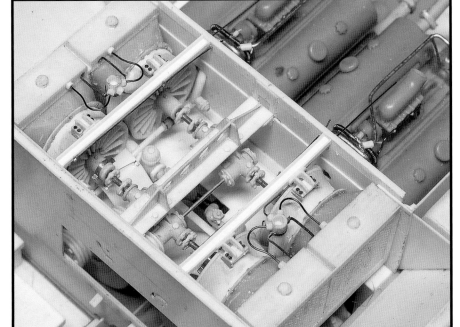

# 2

# ENGINES

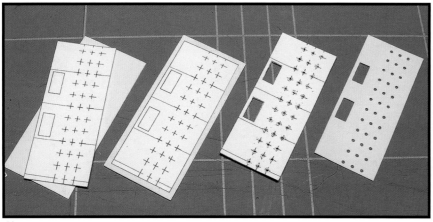

**Above** After having determined the dimensions of the e-motors and generators I made a template for all holes on my pc. These were printed on paper and glued with white glue on sheets of styrene. After the holes were made the paper was removed and the sheets were wrapped around a pre made tube to make the housings. Four are made, two generators and two e-motors.

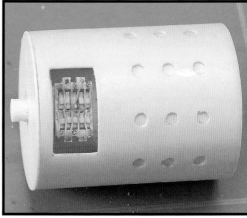

**Above** On the e-motors the contact brushes are visible. One holder with brushes is made for a master that was then used to cast a total of 12 units, six for each motor.

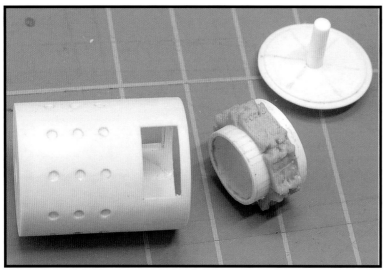

**Above** Six brush holders are cemented on a piece of tubing and the assembly is fitted inside the housing. The holes on the housing still need to have the bolt detail added.

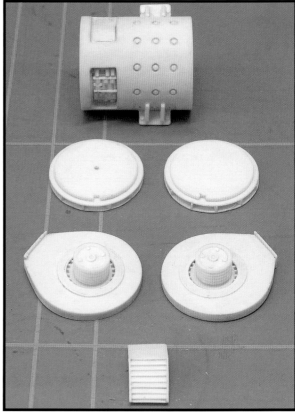

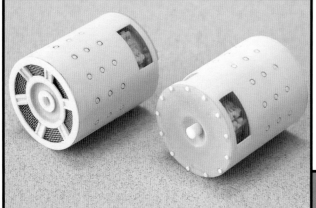

**Above** The generators are different from the e-motors in having a cool air intake ring on the rear and a cyclone fan on the front. How this cyclone fan looked in real is unknown. Inside the surviving Elefant it's difficult to photograph this area and most of the sheet metal hasn't survived time. What I've made is based on two wartime photographs that show one of the engine/generator assemblies being hoisted out, or into, a Ferdinand.

**Above** The e-motors would look like this. The side with the mesh is attached to the clutch/brake assembly and the other side connects to the final drive on the hull side.
.

**Right** The main power unit, Maybach HL120 TRM and Siemens generator. The service opening for the brushes will be covered by the cover with louvers.

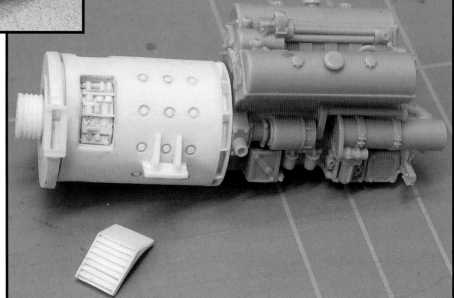

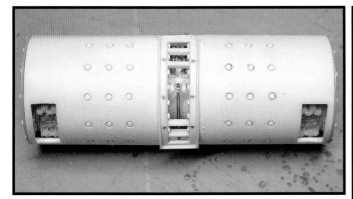

**Above** The e-motors connected by the clutch/brake unit. This unit contains a limited slip clutch for each motor and a dual band type parking brake.

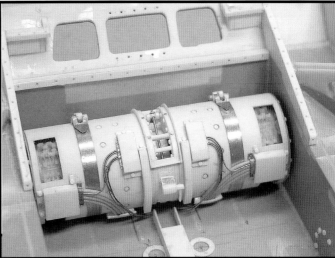

**Above** The e-motors wired up and fitted in the hull.

**Left** The detailed engine/generator units. The grey resin Maybach HL120 TRM engines come from CMK.

**Below** The units fitted inside the hull. Also note the shielding that protects the fuel tanks. The cyclone fans are connected to the ducts inside the hull by smaller connecting ducts. They couldn't be reached in the real vehicle but D656/3 showed a similar connecting duct as on the model.

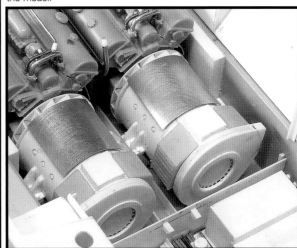

**Above** At the rear of the Maybach engines the auxiliary generators are mounted an a specially designed bracket. Since these generators are now behind the engine instead of mounted on them there are belt tensioners attached to the engine. On the left is the air compressor for the air assisted brakes. Also the drive shafts to the fans are added here.

**Above** The compartment with resistors and cooling fans for the engine compartment. On the right an acces panel in the floor duct to the bolts for the rear suspension unit swing axle. The swingarm axles for the left and right rear swingarm units are most accessable, but for the left and right centre units the engines and generators would need to be removed. To remove the engines and generators the cooling unit with radiators need tob e taken out but only after the superstructure with main gun has been taken from the vehicle.

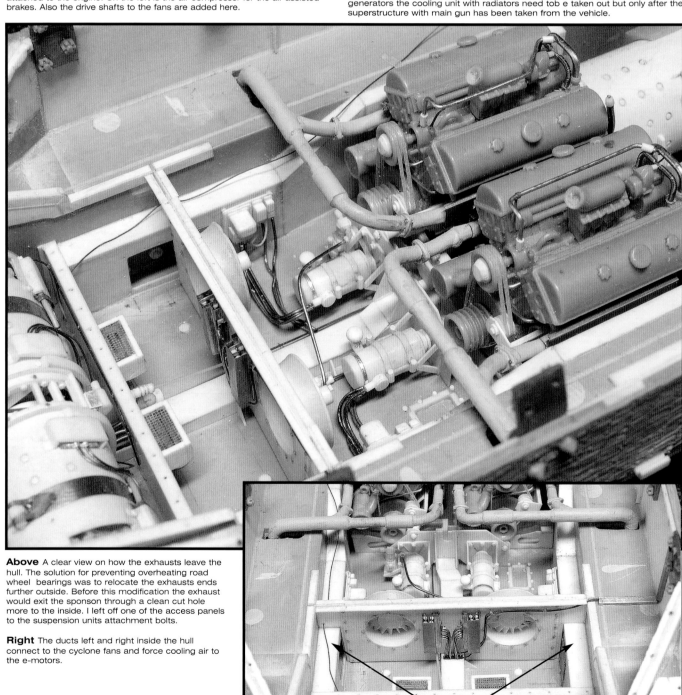

**Above** A clear view on how the exhausts leave the hull. The solution for preventing overheating road wheel bearings was to relocate the exhausts ends further outside. Before this modification the exhaust would exit the sponson through a clean cut hole more to the inside. I left off one of the access panels to the suspension units attachment bolts.

**Right** The ducts left and right inside the hull connect to the cyclone fans and force cooling air to the e-motors.

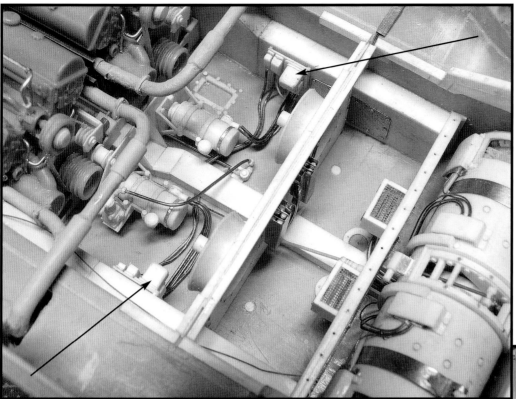

**Left** Fitted onto the side ducts are the Reglerschalter (Voltage regulator box)and Entstörer (Electronic noise suppressor box), a set on both sides, one for each engine.

**Right** With large parts of the ducts being collapsed inside the reference vehicle and a big pile of rubble on the floor it's not clear how the wiring for the Reglerschalter and Entstörer ran but seemingly it was on the floor.

**Below** The two cables leading to the sponson and up along the hull side provide electric power to the fighting compartment.

**Below Right** Another view of the rear of the hull.

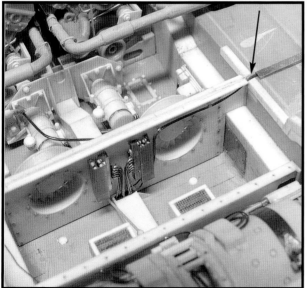

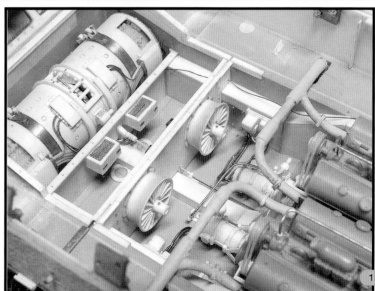

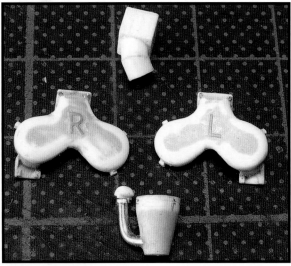

**Left** The air intake manifolds for the Mahle airfilters originate from the Stug-III. There is a left and right half bolted onto a manifold. The pieces are mirrored images and have letters casted on top, R and L, these are made with stretched sprue. The filter housing is made with Magic Sculpt on a styrene base that is sanded to shape. These are the masters for casting the desired numbers.

**Right** The manifold parts together. All will be supported on three metal legs and a flexible duct connects to the engines.

**Below** The cast copies of the air filter assemblies in their locations in the vehicle, also showing the ducts to the engines. Some smaller details still needs to be added.

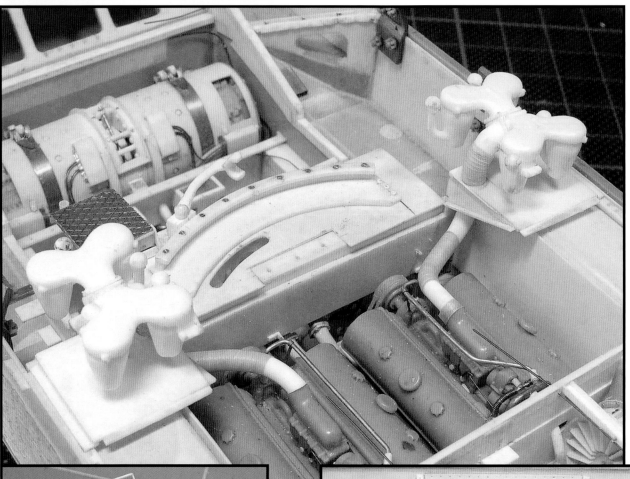

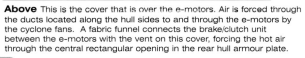

**Above** This is the cover that is over the e-motors. Air is forced through the ducts located along the hull sides to and through the e-motors by the cyclone fans. A fabric funnel connects the brake/clutch unit between the e-motors with the vent on this cover, forcing the hot air through the central rectangular opening in the rear hull armour plate.

**Above** Over this cover will be the slanted floor. Hot air is forced out of the engine compartment by the two fans in the dividing wall, guided between this cover and the slanted floor, and leaving the vehicle through the openings in the rear armour.

**Above** A look at the fan drive gears. The two petrol engines drive a total of six of these fans, and two generators with cyclone fans. All together consuming considerable horsepower.

**Left** One of the fans that extract hot air from the engine compartment.

**Below Left** The two coolant return hoses going in-between the two generators. The lhs generator is partially visible here.

**Above Right** A view on the LHS fans.

**Left** The RHS valve and coolant transfer connections with a red coloured cap. In the top right is the connection for the return line having a blue cap.

**Below** This shows the length of the drive belts. Just visible is the top of the cyclone fan housing.

**Left** A view under the deck plate, behind the fans the two radiators.

**Above** Manufacturers plate on the radiator.

**Right** Outboard side of the LHS radiators, on the right a 9mm thick protection plate over the fuel tank.

**Below** Two views of the intakes for the radiator.

**Above** A rear view of one of the two Maybach HL120 TRM engines. The blue drum is the oilcooler that connects with a hose to the radiators

**Left** Two views looking under the traversing platform showing the crank start linkages and exhausts for the pair of Maybach engines.

**Below** The RHS Maybach engine. Lying on the drive belts is a piece of the elevation gear concertina sleeve. On the cylinder head a piece of the air intake tubing.

**Top** The Siemens e-motors are secured to the hull with a wide steel band. Note the interlocks of the armoured vent cover not being welded here.

**Above** Each motor has a carrier with six brush holders, each with 10 contact brushes. The carrier could rotate each holder to the opening for inspection or work.

**Right** Inside the assembly that connects the two motors are the limited slip clutches and the parking brake.

**Bottom Right** Under the slanted floor is a cover that guides hot air from the e-motors out of the vehicle through the duct that is bolted onto it. In-between this cover and the slanted floor hot air from the engine compartment is vented.

**Below** The framing on the underside for the fabric funnel that connected to the e-motor.

**Above** A look under the Brücke with the twin Maybachs. In the foreground is the belt driven water pump. Left is the rear of the vehicle.

**Above** Floor and cover had felt seals all around. In the right corner is the access panel to the brushes of the e-motor.

**Above** The propeller shaft from the Maybach engine that drives the fan. On its left the air compressor pump, on the right one of the dynamos, moved there from the engine block because of the limited space due to the air ducts running along each side of the hull interior.

**Above** The resistors in the compartment in front of the e-motors. Seemingly these are brake resistors. When the vehicle slows down the e-motors will start to generate electricity. The brake resistors convert this electric energy into thermal energy that can be vented out of this compartment.

# 3

# DRIVER'S COMPARTMENT

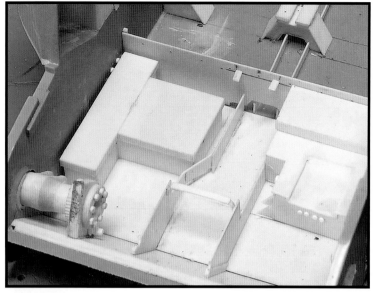

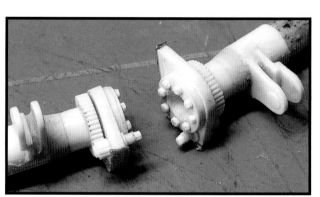

**Left** The layout of the bow compartment floor, occupied by the Driver and Radio Operator. The boxes on the right side hold a total of four batteries. The box on the Driver's side contains the brake cylinder for the brake foot pedal and electrical components for steering.

**Below** The pair of track tensioners minus the threaded adjuster rods with nuts which are mounted in between the pair of brackets. Visible on the left unit are the adjustment gears.

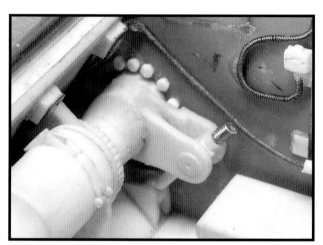

**Above** The completed and installed tensioner unit with the brake line attached. To adjust track tension the nuts on the rods needed to be turned loose. Than a small gear wheel could be turned with a wrench to rotate the tensioner in the desired direction. At the correct tension the two nuts on the threaded rod needed to tightened to hold the tensioner in position.

**Above** A better view on the threaded rod in place on top of the adjuster in position in the hull.

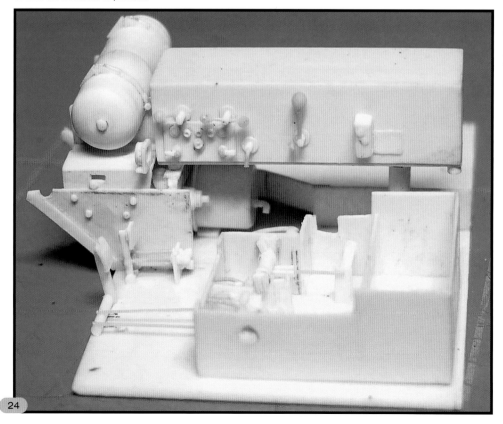

**Left** To make work easier the floor which holds all components was constructed so that it was removable. Added here is the Driver's centre console with assorted switches, in front of which is the compressed air tank for the power brakes. Under the tank are the two air-assisted master brake cylinders.

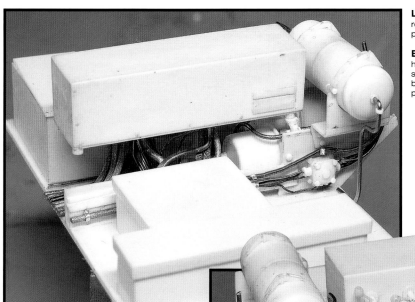

**Left** This shows the Radio Operator's side and I tried to replicate all the wiring and associated plumbing as much as possible.

**Below** Back to the Driver's side with wooden flooring and handbrake lever are added, and showing the plumbing on this side. The rear of the centre console is supported in the vehicle by brackets on the lower part of the firewall absent from this picture.

**Below** The frontal glacis armour. A remainder of VK.4501 (P) design are the four vision holes drilled in the armour on the Driver's side and the two vertical cut offs in the centre. For the Jagdpanzer additional square armour, threaded blocks are welded onto the inner face, and for the ball mount required on the Elefant a hole was crudely torch-cut into the original armour. Also note the protruding interlocks.

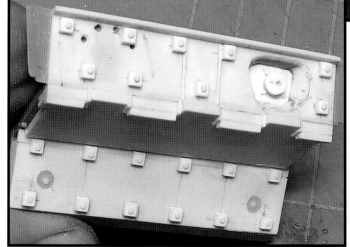

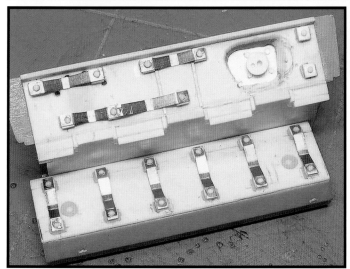

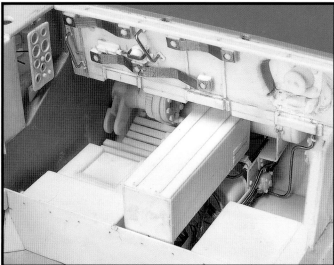

**Left** Apparently to prevent the threaded blocks from flying through the compartment after a direct hit the blocks have retaining strips welded onto them.

**Above** The floor assembly and frontal armour are fitted into the hull along with the massive track tensioners and the driver's instrument panel on the left side of the hull.

**Left** Also note the bell and Maschinentelegraph (direction indicator) located in front of the driver. A Bowden cable leads to a lever at the commanders position and will be added later.

**Above** The Driver's seat. It was adjustable in two positions, up or down. To move upwards it was spring assisted.

**Left** The lower part of the compartment firewall which is fixed to the hulll. On it are the two fuel filters, valves and lines coming from the fuel tanks and at the top centre are the brackets to support the back of the Driver's console.

**Below** The lower firewall section fitted in place and the fuel lines connected to the fuel tanks. The floor assembly is still removable by sliding it out to the front.

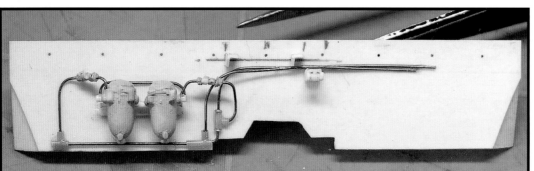

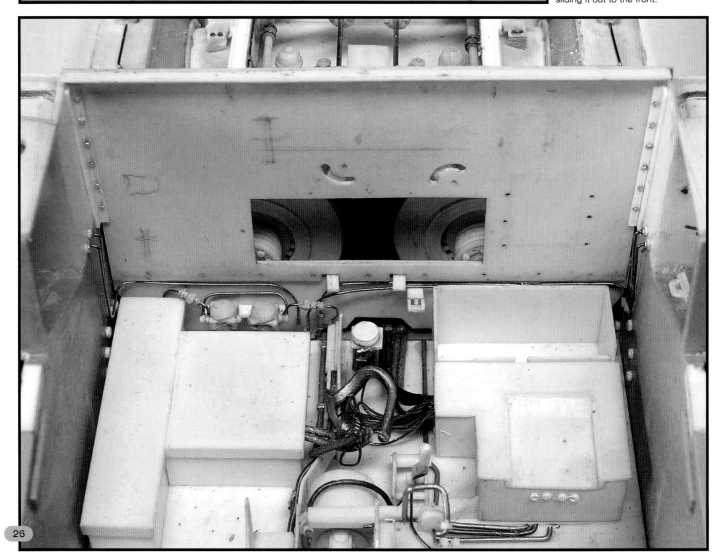

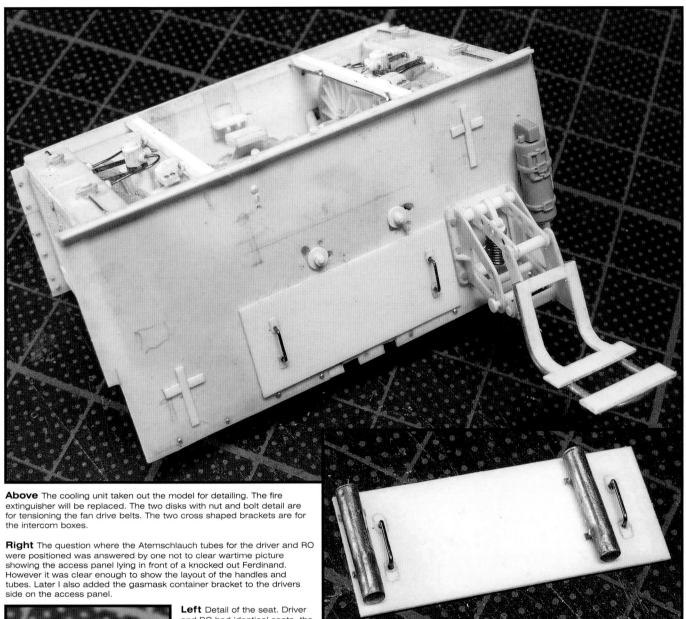

**Above** The cooling unit taken out the model for detailing. The fire extinguisher will be replaced. The two disks with nut and bolt detail are for tensioning the fan drive belts. The two cross shaped brackets are for the intercom boxes.

**Right** The question where the Atemschlauch tubes for the driver and RO were positioned was answered by one not to clear wartime picture showing the access panel lying in front of a knocked out Ferdinand. However it was clear enough to show the layout of the handles and tubes. Later I also added the gasmask container bracket to the drivers side on the access panel.

**Left** Detail of the seat. Driver and RO had identical seats, the type also used in other German AFVs.

**Below Left** The radio sets were mounted under the glacis plate. This is the Aber set without the radio set facias fitted.

**Below** Mounted inside the vehicle. On the right are the mounting brackets for the transformers which power the radios.

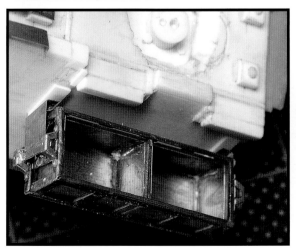

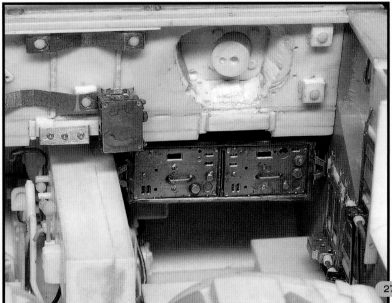

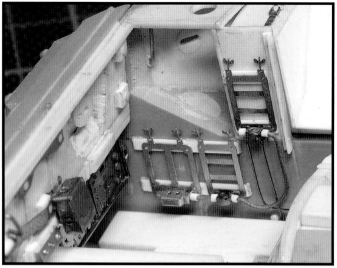

**Above** The mounting brackets for the transformers, also from the Aber set.

**Above** The transformer covers are replaced by more correct scratch built covers.

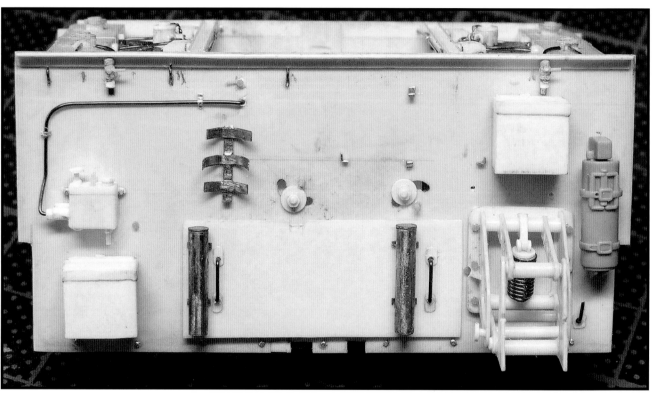

**Above** The completed firewall on the front of the cooling unit which forms the back of the bow compartment.

**Below** Here it is fitted into the hull.

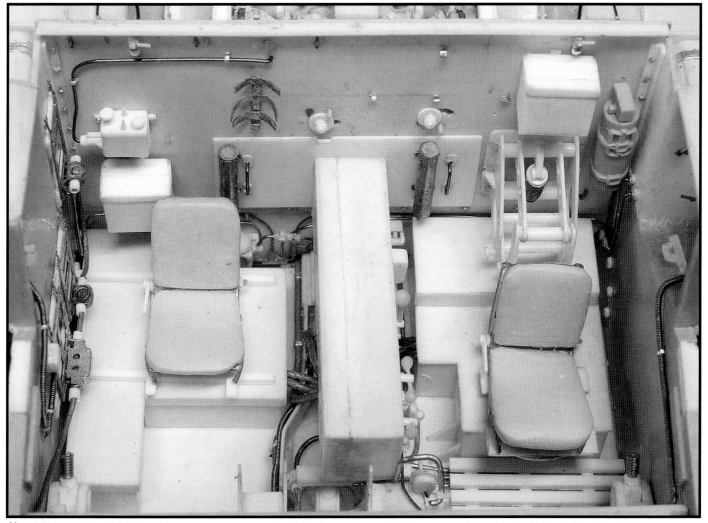

**Above** The completed Driver/Radio Operator's compartment. The Radio Operator's seat is fitted on a metal frame that also holds the lids of the battery boxes.

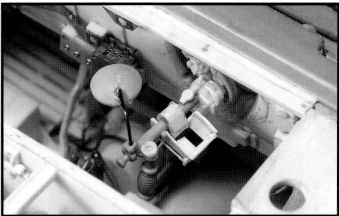

**Above** The Dragon MG-34 mount received missing detail.

**Left** The springs to counterbalance the weight of the hatches are mounted to the deck plate.

**Below** Detail on the drivers hatch. The rain cover surrounding the hatch is recessed and closes over the strip surrounding the hatch opening. In my reference I have seen no evidence of rubber sealings used on any of the hatches.

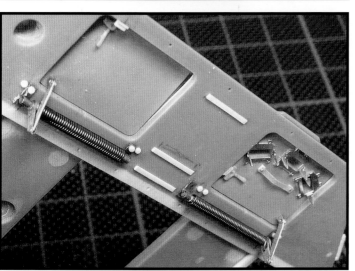

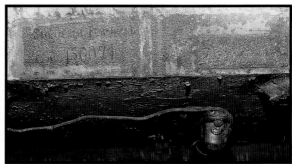

**Above** The stamping on the interlock in front of the driver reads: Stu. Gesch. Ferdinand F. Nr. 150071 – Sturmgeschütz Ferdinand, Fahrgestell Nr. 150071.

**Below left** Viewing from the Radio Operator's position towards the Driver's position. On the right against the frontal armour the Maschinentelegraph with bell.

**Below** The adjustable mechanism for the drivers seat. On the ceiling the massive spring that counters the weight of the hatch.

**Above** Electric wiring and the two oil pressure lines that once were connected to the instrument panel. Note the rubber suspension points for the panel, the same as used for radio sets. Note the Ferdinand vision slit having been plated over and welded shut. **Below** Looking down through the drivers hatch.

**Above** The back rest of the drivers seat is missing. The lever on the firewall at the right of the seat is for operating the Spaltfilter (edge type oil filters). Under the seat the box with master brake cylinders and electrics for steering (Fahrschalter) Of interest, steering was achieved using the e-motors. Pulling a steering lever slowed down the e-motor on the corresponding side. By pulling the lever further to a certain position the mechanical brake was activated. Pulling the levers to the rear with the buttons on the handles pushed, activated reverse drive.

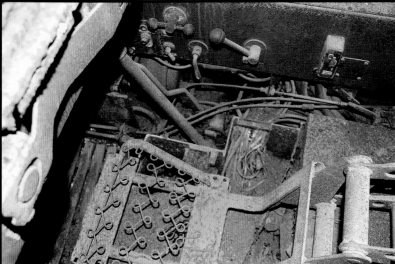

**Above & right** Two views of the driver's controls on the centre console.

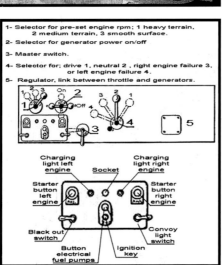

1- Selector for pre-set engine rpm; 1 heavy terrain, 2 medium terrain, 3 smooth surface.

2- Selector for generator power on/off

3- Master switch.

4- Selector for; drive 1, neutral 2 , right engine failure 3, or left engine failure 4.

5- Regulator, link between throttle and generators.

Charging light left engine

Charging light right engine

Socket

Starter button left engine

Starter button right engine

Black out switch

Convoy light switch

Button electrical fuel pumps

Ignition key

**Left** The track tensioner unit. The small hand wheel is not part of the unit. Just visible is the hydraulic line entering the unit on top the right. The brake pedal activated both air assisted hydraulic brakes. Note the rough demarcation between the Grey-Green and Ivory.

**Below** Looking through the opening in the firewall shows the front of the LHS generator. The belts drive the radiators' fans. The access panel is missing on this vehicle.

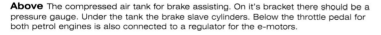

**Above** The compressed air tank for brake assisting. On it's bracket there should be a pressure gauge. Under the tank the brake slave cylinders. Below the throttle pedal for both petrol engines is also connected to a regulator for the e-motors.

**Right** A view across the compartment from the Radio Operator's position. The remains of the intercom box Kasten Pz.N.20 are visible in the top right of this picture.

**Above** The two fuel filters with their valves. The thick layer of debris has been removed here and now we can just see on the floor how the four batteries were positioned. Two along the hull side and two next to them.

**Above** View beneath the console, towards the firewall. In the foreground is one of the battery cables.

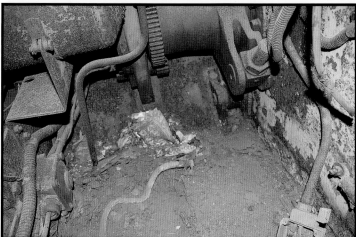

**Above** The front corner of the bow with the track tensioner and on the left the compressed air cylinder On the right with red stencilling is the antenna connection box and behind it the RHS bracket for the radio rack.

**Left** Just visible at the underside of the track tensioner unit is the small gear for adjusting the unit. On the right of the unit against the side armour the securing rod and nut.

**Above** The compressed air tank with it's feed line coming from the air compressor in the rear of the vehicle.

**Right** Fuses on the RHS of the console. Under the console one of the brake slave cylinders.

**Above** Looking up at the glacis plate at the Radio Operator's position. The bracket next to the interlock is for the radio rack.

**Right** A further view of the bow and track tensioning mechansim.

**Above** The side wall on the Radio Operator's side of the hull showing the remains of the mount for the MG-34 and the mounting brakets fro the missing transformers.

**Right** The three frames onto which the transformers were mounted. Under the left frame is one of the battery ground cables bolted onto the hull wall.

**Right** On the roof behind the hatch the antenna mount can be seen. On the firewall is the Anlasskraftstof (cold start primer pump) for the Maybach engine. On the right is a gasmask container bracket. Behind the hatch springa piece of felt sealer has come loose from the top of the firewall.

# 4

# FIGHTING COMPARTMENT

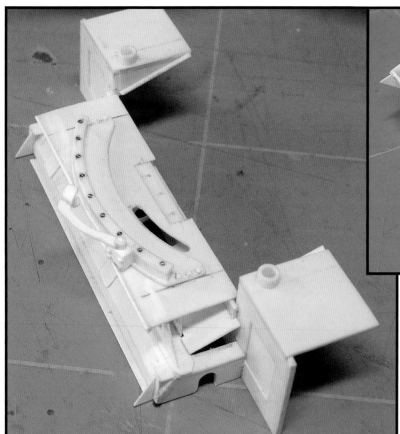

**Left** The gun traverse platform.

**Above** The underside of the platform. The two brass rods are for the engine hand crank mechanism.

**Left** The two main parts that hold the main gun. The traversing platform and the bridge (Brücke) with a connecting piece called Strebe. On the bridge the ball pivot for the carriage is bolted (not added yet)

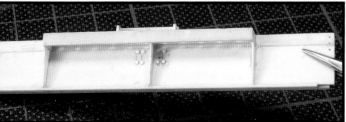

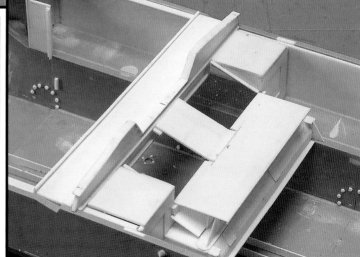

**Above** The underside of the bridge. The eight bolts are for the ball pivot.

**Right** The bridge, platform and brace fitted in the vehicle.

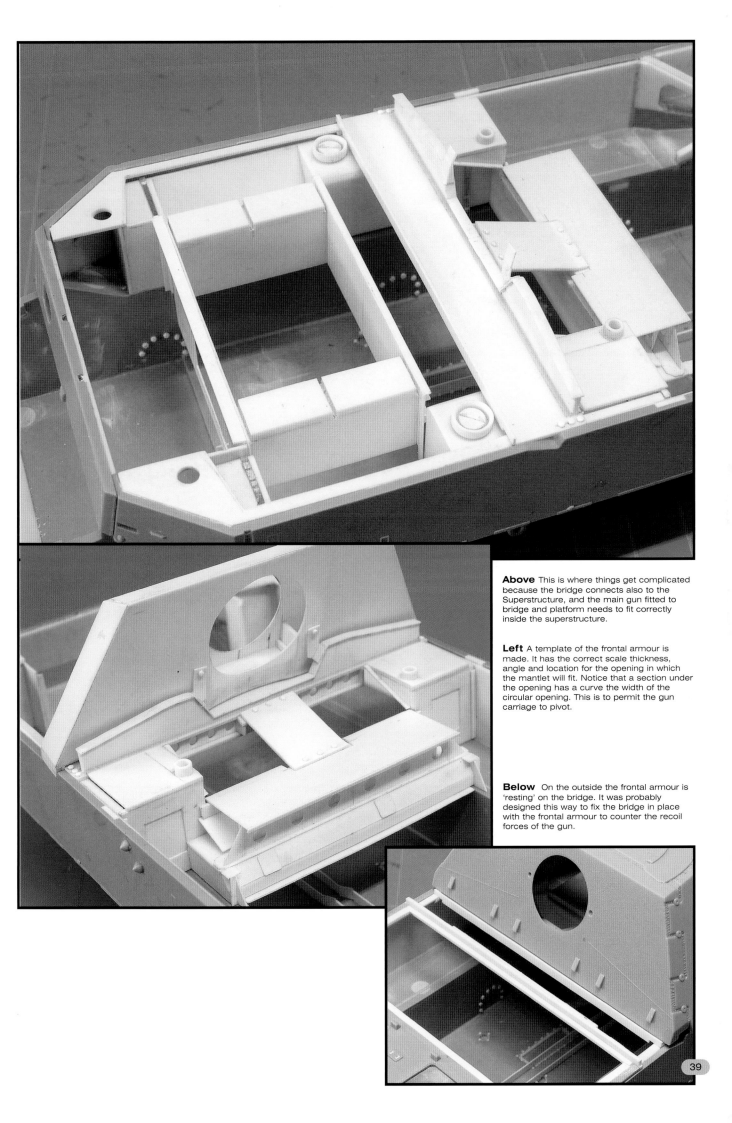

**Above** This is where things get complicated because the bridge connects also to the Superstructure, and the main gun fitted to bridge and platform needs to fit correctly inside the superstructure.

**Left** A template of the frontal armour is made. It has the correct scale thickness, angle and location for the opening in which the mantlet will fit. Notice that a section under the opening has a curve the width of the circular opening. This is to permit the gun carriage to pivot.

**Below** On the outside the frontal armour is 'resting' on the bridge. It was probably designed this way to fix the bridge in place with the frontal armour to counter the recoil forces of the gun.

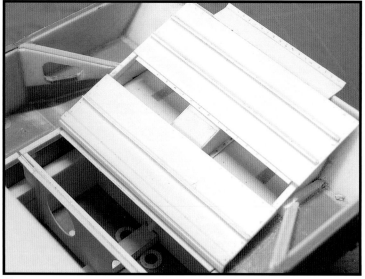

**Above** The slanted floor is made out of two sections and bolted to the vehicle along the sides. Hot air from the engine compartment is forced underneath it and vented out the vehicle. In real everything was sealed with felt strips.

**Above** On the front of the dividing wall with fans the supporting frame for the floor panels is added.

**Above** The strip at the front of this frame connects with the traversing platform. At the rear the panels rest on a strip attached to the slanted floor part.

**Left** On the slanted floor are pieces of a U-shaped profile, the possible use of them will be explained later.

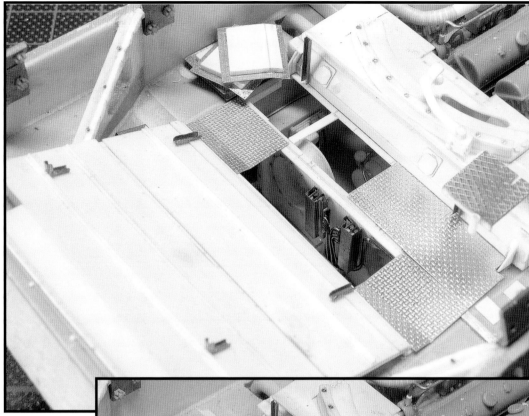

**Above & Right** Floor panels are added using photoetched treadplate. The real tiles are insulated with rock wool.

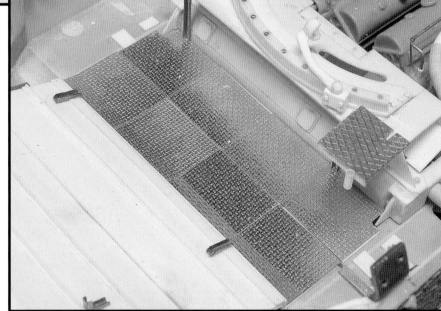

**Below & Right** The Commander's seat and foot rest with some spring detail added.

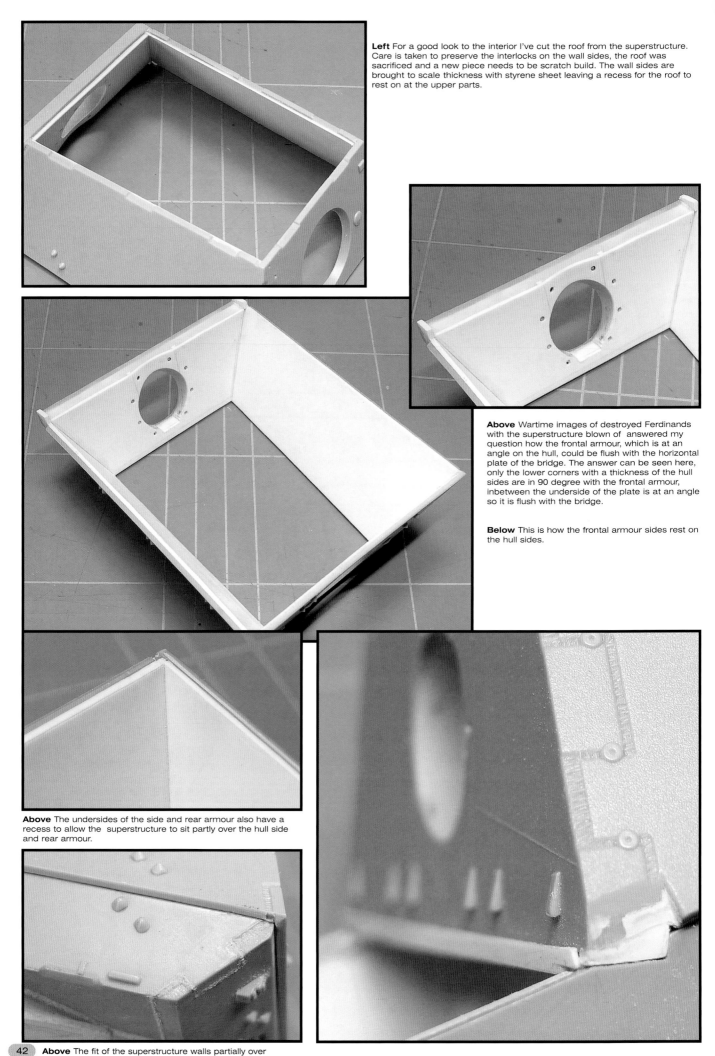

**Left** For a good look to the interior I've cut the roof from the superstructure. Care is taken to preserve the interlocks on the wall sides, the roof was sacrificed and a new piece needs to be scratch build. The wall sides are brought to scale thickness with styrene sheet leaving a recess for the roof to rest on at the upper parts.

**Above** Wartime images of destroyed Ferdinands with the superstructure blown of answered my question how the frontal armour, which is at an angle on the hull, could be flush with the horizontal plate of the bridge. The answer can be seen here, only the lower corners with a thickness of the hull sides are in 90 degree with the frontal armour, inbetween the underside of the plate is at an angle so it is flush with the bridge.

**Below** This is how the frontal armour sides rest on the hull sides.

**Above** The undersides of the side and rear armour also have a recess to allow the superstructure to sit partly over the hull side and rear armour.

**Above** The fit of the superstructure walls partially over the hull walls.

**Above** Test fitting things. Frontal armour and bridge are good.

**Left** Since my kit has the pistol port plugs moulded on these are removed and the holes drilled out. First with a drill bit the size for the inner sides, than with a drill bit slightly larger for the outsides preventing not to go through the smaller interior holes. Than I filled the sides of the hole with Magic Sculpt and sculpted the holes until they were tapered. Also the holes in the top corners are drilled out. Since the kit welds lie to deep I've redone them with Magic Sculpt.

**Below Left** The new roof from styrene sheet.

**Below** Roof welds are added. Before applying Magic Sculpt to make the welds a thin coat of Vaseline is applied to the areas of the wall where the roof rests on.

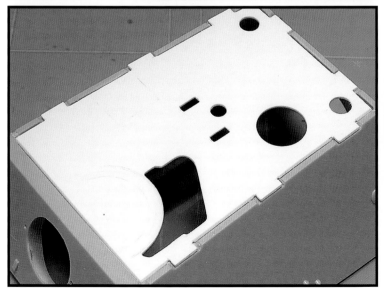

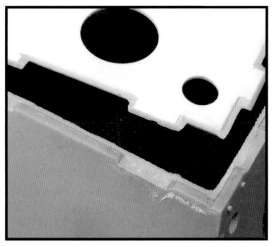

**Above** Once the Magic Sculpt is completely set a few gentle taps make the roof with welds come loose from the walls.

**Above** The inner side with all welds applied.

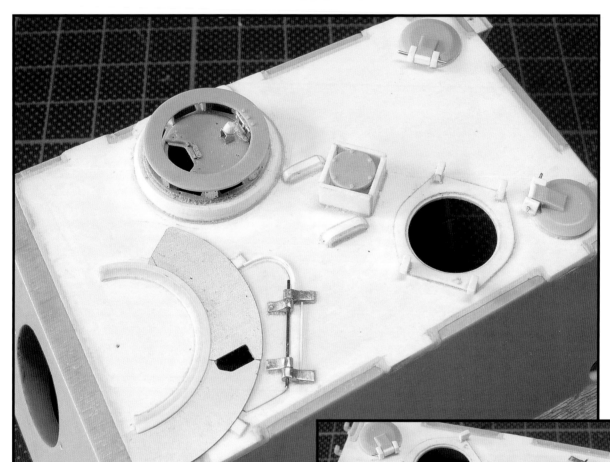

**Above** Except for the hatches everything on the roof needed to be scratch build. Since the interior is going to be detailed a new commanders cupola is made, also originating from the Stug-III.

**Above** All hatches are movable and received some detail, mostly welds.

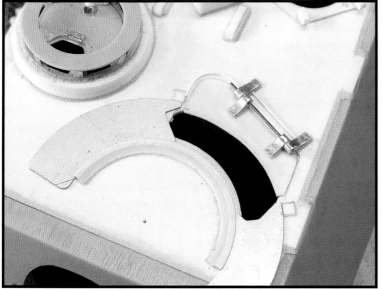

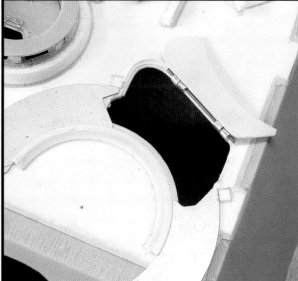

**Above** On most models the hinged gun sight hatch is on top of the roof whilst it should be flush with the top of the roof being partially under the sliding covers.

**Above Right** To open the hatch the sliding covers needed to be opened all the way.

**Right** The detailed loaders hatch and periscope hatch.

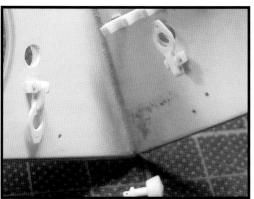

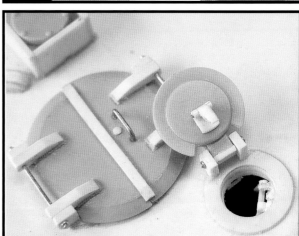

**Above** The pistol port locks are movable.

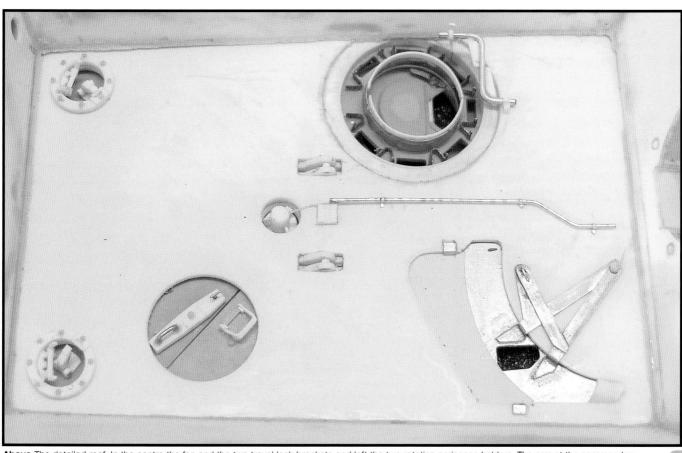

**Above** The detailed roof. In the centre the fan and the two travel lock brackets and left the two rotating periscope holders. The arm at the commanders cupola is for attaching Scherenfernrohr (Scissors periscope).

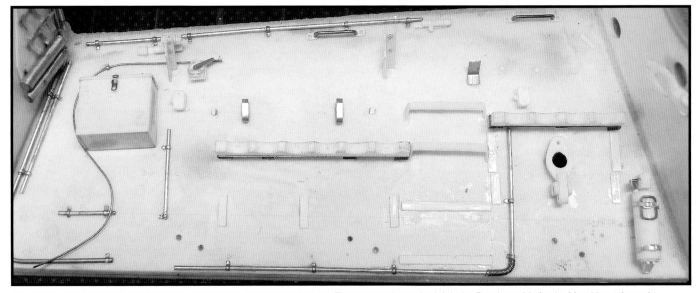

**Above** The rhs wall with all detail only the ammo racks are not complete yet. The copper wire on the left is the Bowden cable for the Maschinentelegraph (direction indicator) between commander and driver.

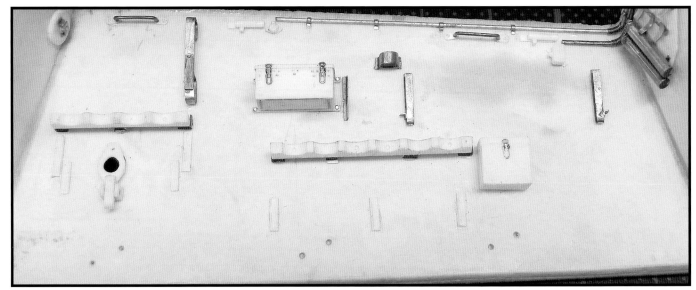

**Above** The LHS wall.

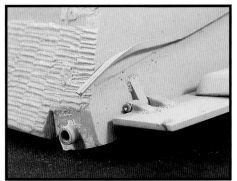

**Above** The tube in the corner is part of the connection between superstructure and hull.

**Left** Newly made pistol port plugs with chain.

**Above** The securing plates that hold the superstructure to the hull, made from lead sheet. Three on each side and two on the rear.

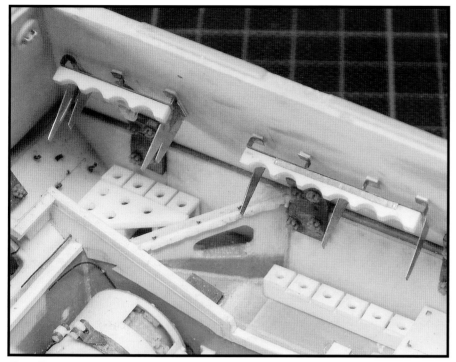

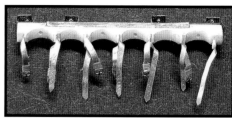

**Above** The straps to secure the rounds of ammo, this is the front storage. Straps are made from thin aluminium packaging foil.

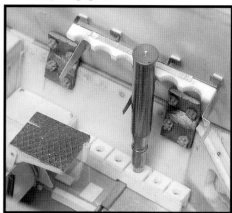

**Above** The round would be secured by straps and a metal strip that hinges between the brass brackets. A total of 26 rounds could be stored this way. Later in the build we find out some other possible ways to store rounds.

**Above** The ammo storage. Strangely the rear storage has only brackets to secure 7 rounds. If rounds would be placed in the inner two floor support holes they needed to be secured by other means.

**Right** The same on the right side.

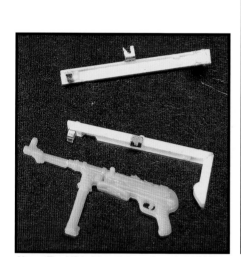

**Above** The MP holders, two on the rear wall left and right of the circular hatch.

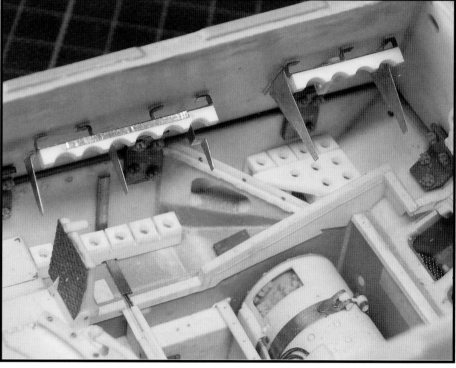

**Left** The Montageluke (circular hatch) was used to mount/dismount the main gun. The two top latches are 'unlocked', to lock the hatch they swivel upwards.

**Right** Scratch build fire extinguishers, one goes next to the drivers seat the other in the fighting compartment

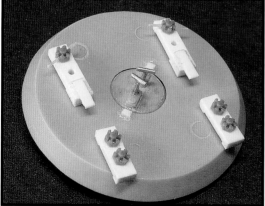

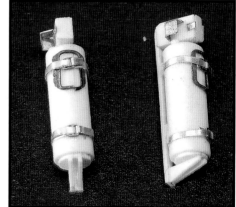

**Above** One of the eight Mahle air filters.

**Right** Underside of the air filter unit

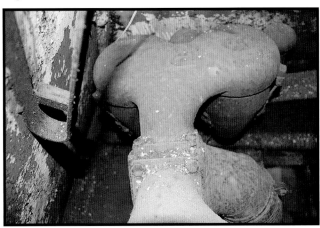

**Above** Top view of the air filter unit.

**Right** The stencilling on the large box just above the air filters on the commander's side states Funkzubehör (Radio equipment; headphone and throat microphone).

**Below** A view looking forward from the gunner's position showing the air filters on the LHS. Visible are the supporting frame legs and the flexible metal tubing that connects to the air intake on the Maybach engine.

**Above** On the sponson are stacked a few of the insulated floor panels with the remains of the gunners seat, backrest and another air filter on top. Above this is one of the ammunition stowage racks.

**Above** In the left upper corner a mounting plate with two Atemschlauch (Breathing tubes) storage tubes and gasmask container brackets. Barely visible but still present: the stenciling Atemschlauch and Gasmasken.

**Right** The ammo bracket in the left rear corner. On the rear wall one of the two MP40 stowage brackets.

**Below** The box for the spare persicopes with it's interior in a remarkably good condition.

**Right** The massive circular hatch with on each side a pistol port, MP brackets and periscopes brackets.

49

**Above** One of the 'locks' on the hatch.

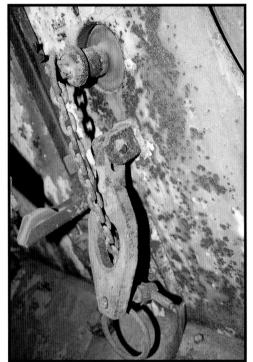

**Left** One of the pistol port plugs in position with its retainer.

**Above & Right** The same pistol port plug released to hang outside by its chain.

**Below Left** The pivoting periscope mount in the rhs rear corner.

**Below Right** One of the superstructure interior lights. A different design to those found in the Driver's compartment.

**Above** The ammo rack in the RHS rear corner. Just above it the intercom box for the loader. On the right in the lower corner a fire extinguisher bracket.

**Above** Another view of RHS rear corner. Note the awkwardly positioned pistol port behind the ammunition rack.

**Below** Looking forward on the RHS around the breech towards the Commander's position.

**Above** The Commander's saddle on it's hinged platform with the other set of air filters behind it.

**Below** The Kasten Pz. Nr. 6a is mounted just below the air filters ahead of the Commander.

**Above Left** The commanders cupola with in front of it the support for the scissors periscope. Under it and against the side armour is the lever for the Maschinentelegraph.

**Left** Notice the circular cut out in the roof for the cupola. At the rear (left) the cupola sits flush with underside of the roof plate whilst at the front (right) the cupola rests on the roof plate.

**Above** On the side armour the control for the Maschinentelegraph and a bracket for the MG-34 with a small placard.

**Above** On the placard; Fahrgestellnummer 150071

**Left** The wooden supports for the ammo rounds. With the rounds placed upside down the nose ends fit in the holes. Six rounds are stored here, the support with the three holes belongs to the RHS.

**Left** The wooden supports in the LHS corner.

**Top** An overall view of the LHS hull rear corner with the sloped floor and the wooden ammunition racks. The angled section was originally the rear corner of the VK.4501 (P) hull. A hole was cut in it and the torch marks along the top edge show where a deck plate was cut from this section.

**Top** Just visible under the debris are welded on plates for the additional ammo racks.

**Above** A more simple design for the inner rounds.

**Above** A view inside the Kubinka Ferdinand also shows the welded on plates, In the lower right corner the wooden front support for the nose ends of three rounds. Towards the rear the two other plates are visible. Photo courtesy of Per Sonnervik.

**Below** Again the Kubinka Ferdinand showing the rear RHS floor with the checker pattern treadplate sections and the sloped rear section. Photo courtesy of Per Sonnervik.

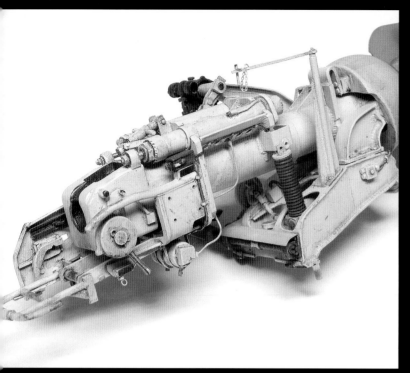

# 5

# MAIN GUN

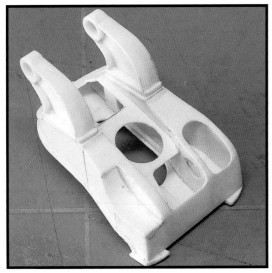

**Above** The carriage for the Kwk.43 L71. The Jagdpanther uses the same carriage so this is good reference.

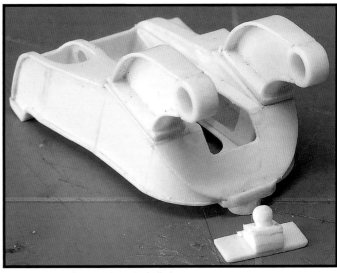

**Above** In front of the carriage the ball pivot.

**Far Right** The mantlet needed some work. The sides are closed and the inner side reworked so that the trunnions will fit. The two extrusions are for fitting the mantlet to the gun tube.

**Right** This is how the mantlet is fixed to the gun tube, bolt detail still needs to be added.

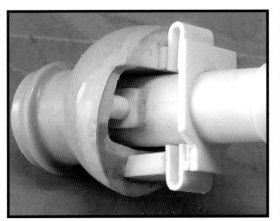

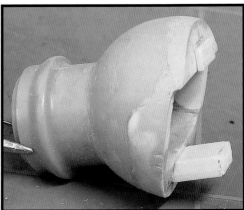

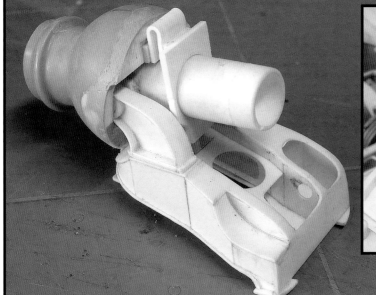

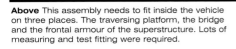

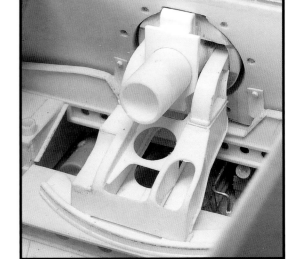

**Above** This assembly needs to fit inside the vehicle on three places. The traversing platform, the bridge and the frontal armour of the superstructure. Lots of measuring and test fitting were required.

**Above Right** Fitting on the platform and bridge.

**Right** Fitting on platform, bridge and with the frontal armour.

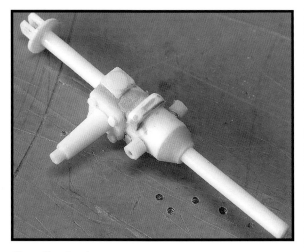

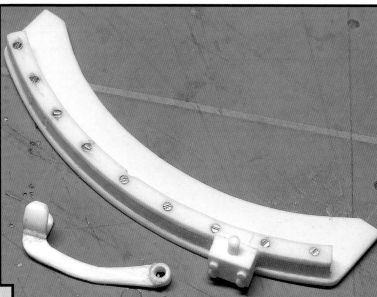

**Above** The elevation gear.

**Right** The Führungswinkel (traversing rail).

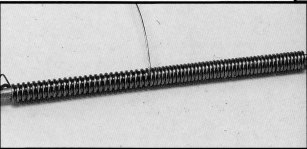

**Above** The threaded rod for the traversing mechanism is made by coiling two different gauges of copper wire around a brass rod. First the thicker wire followed by a thinner wire pulling it between the thicker coils.

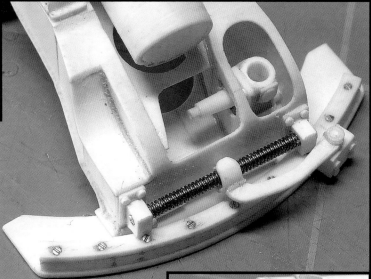

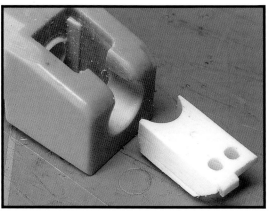

**Above** The traversing gear minus the linkage and hand wheel that go on the left of the carriage.. The arm attached to the rail holds a threaded bushing in which the rod rotates and so moving the carriage left or right.

**Right** The lever for the breech mechanism.

**Above** The reworked breech and new block.

**Below** The only thing that could be used from the kit is the breech. Everything else is scratch build. Here the recuperator on the left and recoil cylinder on the right.

**Below Right** The entire breech guard was also scratchbuilt.

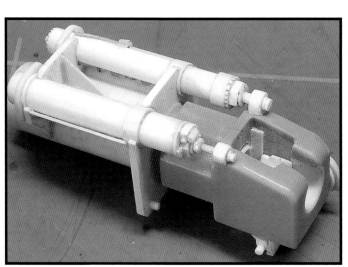

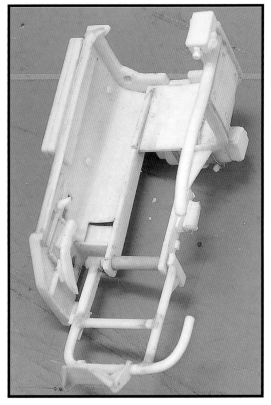

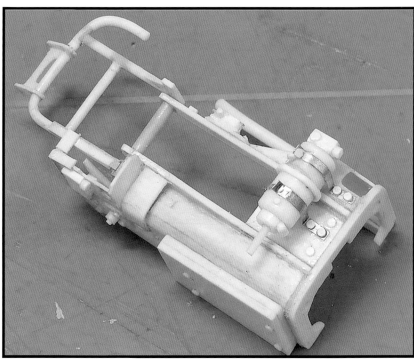

**Above** Added to the underside is the safety cylinder. As part of the safety circuit it was hydraulically connected with the recoil cylinder, if pressure in the recoil cylinder dropped, pressure also dropped in the safety cylinder and a spring opened an electrical contact and the gun could not be fired.

**Above** On top of the guard the loaders safety switch. This switch needed to be reset by the loader after loading a round into the breech.

**Above** The right side with two counter weight plates bolted to the side of the guard.

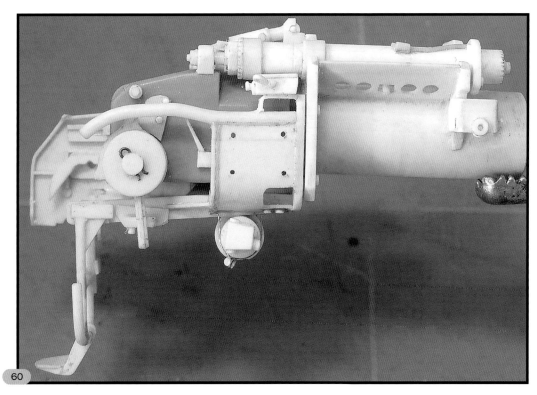

**Left** The gun and guard are brought together, with the guard in the down position another switch was opened to prevent the gun to be fired.

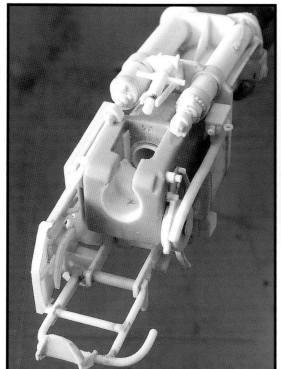

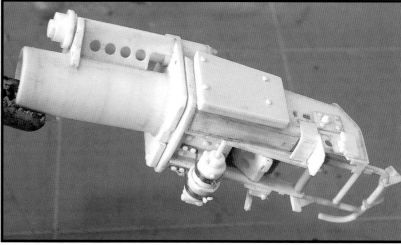

**Above** Two more views of the completed gun guard and shield assembly.

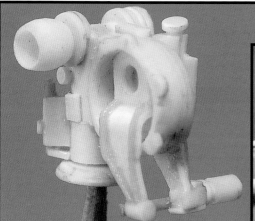

**Above** The mount for the gun sight; Sfl.Z.F.1a.

**Far Right** The elevation gear received it's concertina sleeve. Note the rod from the elevationgear goes through the traversing platform into which a curved slot is provided.

**Right** The completed main gun. The small box on the carriage is connected to the hull with a wire and provides the gun with electrical power.

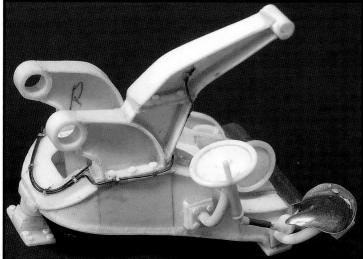

**Left** The completed carriage. The hand wheel is for traversing. The gunners seat was formed out of brass sheet.

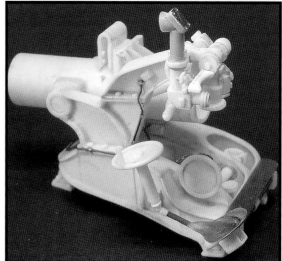

**Left** Quite some work went into the gun sight. Later I decided to leave it off as 102 did not have it mounted when found according to reference pictures.

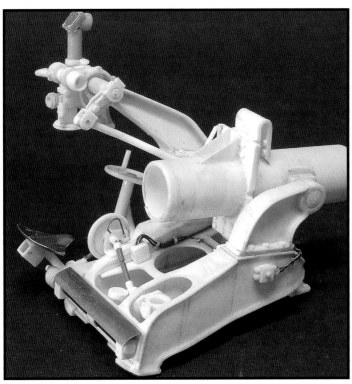

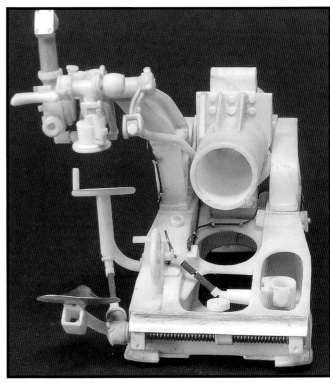

**Above** Visible is the rod that enables the gun sight to move up and down with the gun. From this side in front of the elevation wheel, the trigger handle.

**Above** The linkages from hand wheels to elevation and traversing gears.

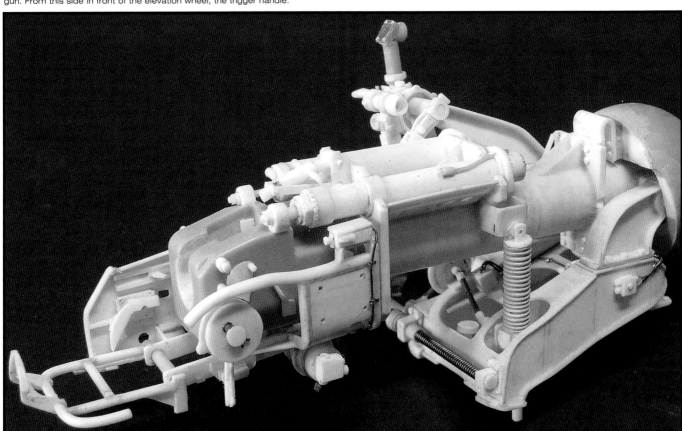

**Above** Views of the completed gun mount

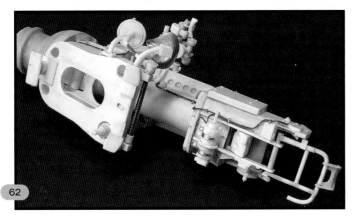

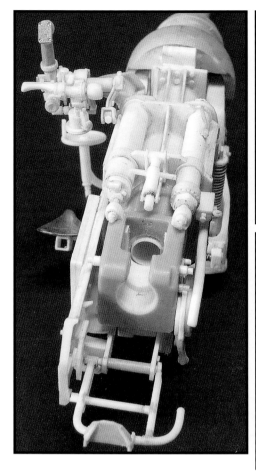

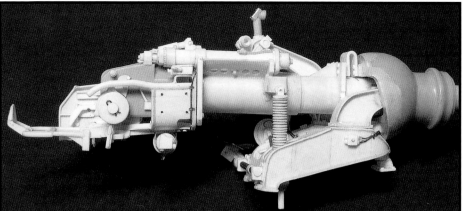

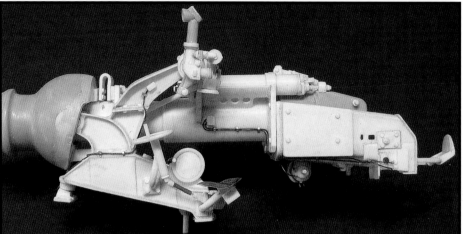

**Below** The completed gun in position in the lower hull.

**Right** The improvements made to both sides of the mantlet shield with added weld detail.

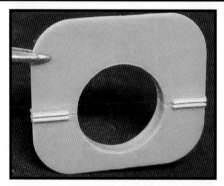

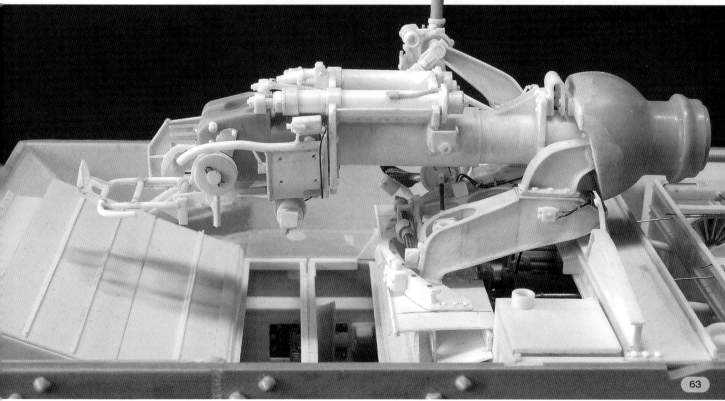

**Above** A look under the main gun. At the top the hydraulic safety cylinder. The two circular recesses are for the starter crancks, the square covers are missing.

**Left** The elevation mechanism. The concertina sleeve still present at it's base. Below it the threaded rod for traversing.

**Below left** The electrical connection between hull and main gun. Note the difference in colours between gun parts and frontal armour.

**Below** The pole on the gun carriage connects to the sliding gun sight covers moving them
in sync with the traversing gun.
The circular spots surrounding the opening in the frontal armour are the bolts that hold the piece of armour surrounding the mantlet on the outer side.

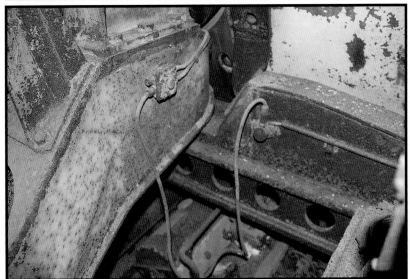

**Above** The LHS trunion. Between Brücke and frontal armour one of the strips that connect the two, the bolt is missing. In the lower right corner the traversing hand wheel.

**Above** The elevation hand wheel with behind it the trigger handle. On the cradle the light to tell the gunner, when on, the gun is loaded with a round and ready for firing.

**Above** One of the items found inside the vehicle is one of the two hooks to support the breech as
part of the travel lock or when lifting the superstructure with gun from the hull.
Between the recoil and recuperator cylinder on top of the main gun is the part that is an
additional fixation rod that is placed between breech and roof to fasten the gun before the
superstructure with the gun would get lifted from the hull.

**Left** The mount for the Sfl.Zf. 1a gun sight. The rod with the "Z"-shaped bend moves the sight up or down in the same degree as the barrel when elevating or depressing.

**Above** A closer look at the mount for the gun sight showing some of the adjusting wheels.

**Left** Looking up at the semi circular opening for the gun sight.

**Below** The mechanism that slide the gun sight covers when traversing the main gun. The strip hanging down from the right is connected with the pole on page 62 and would be connected to the strips that are welded on each cover.

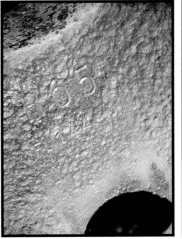

**Above** Markings on the breech block; R65, FL144.

**Left** Markings on the breech; 43 amp. R65, – 53 amp, FL 205, bye.

**Above** On the cradle the loaders safety switch. Behind the switch and on the recoil cylinders the oil line going to the hydraulic safety switch under the beech.

**Right and below** Looking up towards the roof showing the breech mechanism and Commander's cupola which origantes from the Stug III. Remarkably much of the Elfenbein paint is still present on the interior as well as spots of Red Oxyde primer. The extractor fan for some reason received a fresh coat of paint.

# EXTERIOR

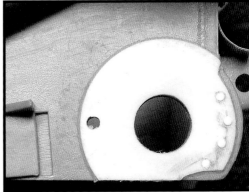

**Above** Welded on plate for the final drive.

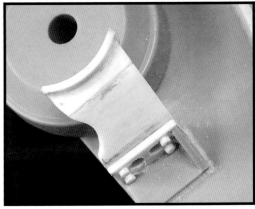

**Above** With all modifications made to the interior the brake sprockets needed new attachment points. This also made it easier to adjust track tensioning later.

**Above** the rear mud scrapers are replaced. Left and right are identical so on the other side the scraper is 'upside-down'.

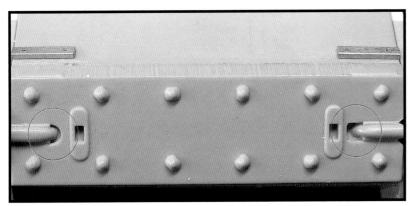

**Above** I noticed a difference in the holes that are in the frontal armour. For some reason during production they changed from round to square. My reference vehicle shows the square holes so both holes were modified. The one on the left still needs to be done.

**Above** The hot air outlet deflectors on the rear. According to German documents hot air was vented with such a force that sometimes drivers couldn't see where they were going due dust being blown under and to the front of the vehicle caused by the shape of the armoured cover. Note the protecting duct for the convoy light wiring.

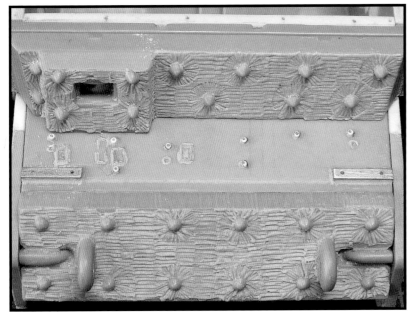

**Above** On the glacis plate nuts are welded to attach spare track links. On the left welds where the jack brackets were when the vehicle was a Ferdinand.

**Above** The Elefant received different fender supports than used on the Ferdinand. My subject still shows marks where the Ferdinand supports were welded.

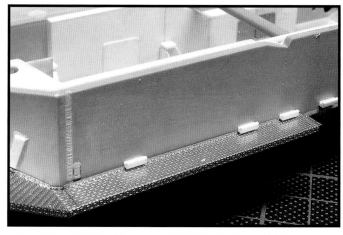

**Above** The white styrene blocks on the hull side are supports for the Ausbaubrücke, a lifting device to remove and fit the suspension units.

**Above** A view on the exhaust protruding the sponson. Against the lower hull where the opening is round is the old position. Also some plugs in the sponson, apparently closed holes from the VK.4501 (P). Also note the blocks for the Ausbaubrücke on the track guide and just above it.

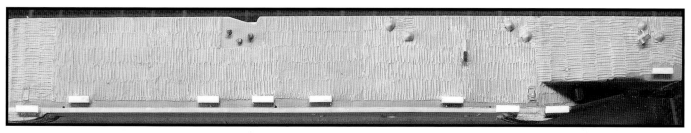

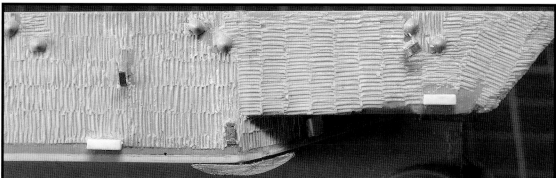

**Above, below and left** A Zimmerit pattern as seen on the Italian front. The well known horizontal pattern and partially a vertical pattern. The pattern is copied as much as possible from wartime photos, or shortly after, of 102. On the right side only a small patch on the rear has the vertical pattern.

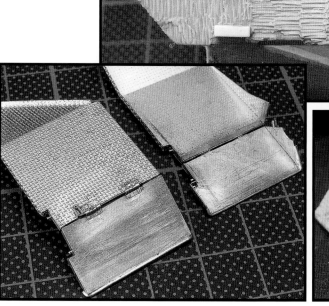

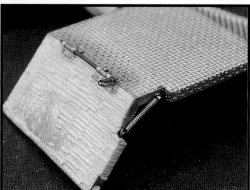

**Left** The fenders are Aber parts. Instructions tell you to bend the front of the mud guards but in real a round bar was welded here. Some copper wire and soldering is used to copy this. Before attaching the spring to the mud guard Zimmerit is applied with Magic Sculp.

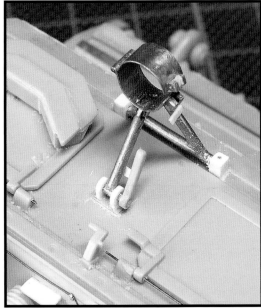

The external travel lock. Partially Aber partially scratch built and movable.

**Below** Wartime pictures of 102 show it had round bars welded to the front openings of the engine compartment hatches, also insides are reworked.

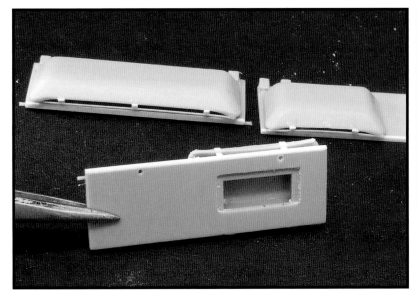

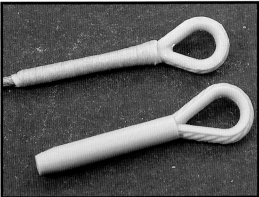

**Above** On top a modified towing cable. Some fabric was wrapped around it and seemingly impregnated. Also the towing eye is modified by adding stretched sprue to the insert to make it wider.

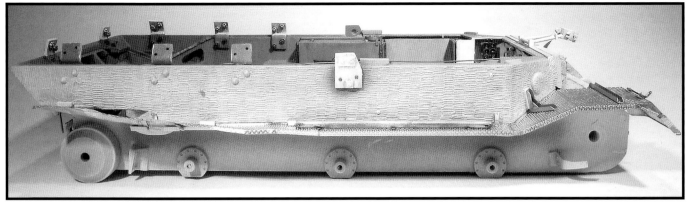

**Above** The completed exterior ready for paint. Fenders on this side of the vehicle had some damage at the rear.

**Above** Zimmerit was applied on each area as close as possible to the original.

**Right** Note the MG34 ball mount is aimed upwarts due to the weight of the MG mount inside.

**Below** The strips on the corners of the armoured vent cover are for the tool box.

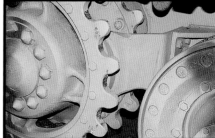

**Above** The rear mud scraper. Also note the rubber behind the holes in the road wheels.

**Above** The RHS front mud scraper.

**Above** On the left side impact damage that also damaged the brakes on this side.

**Above** The right front corner showing partially the massive drum brake.

**Above and below** The rear left corner with protective tubing for the convoy light cable.

**Above** Looking under and in the armoured vent cover. In the centre opening the duct for venting the e-motors is visible.

**Right** The left rear corner. On the lower part of the extended corner some remains of welds. A number of Ferdinands had the gap under the extension and to the mudguard closed with sheet metal.

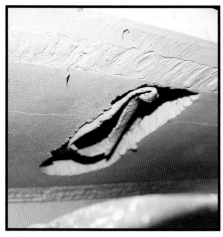

**Above** The opening for the exhaust, note the more circular shape towards the lower hull side, the original location for the exhaust.

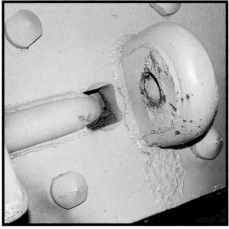

**Above** One of the towing eyes. This is not a massive piece but a rod bent over a steel bushing after which the sides were welded closed. Also note the square hole next to it.

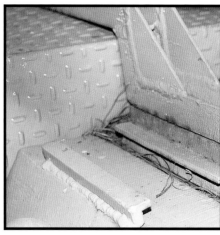

**Above** Note the original tread plate pattern of the fender.

**Above** Close up of a fender support plus bracket for a lifting device to remove and fit the front sprocket and brake parts.

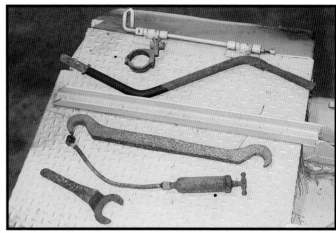

**Above** More of the items found in this vehicle.

**Below** The added armour plates on the frontal armour to house the MG ball mount. The welds at the right of the circular vision port indicate where once a head light was mounted, and the round weld where the power supply cable had entered the hull a little further down. Note stamped part numbers.

**Above** A view on the drivers hatch. Also not how smooth the gun tube is in relation to other parts of the vehicle.

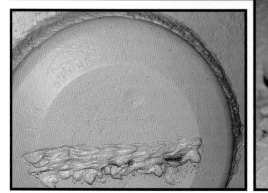

**Left** One of the towing cable brackets.

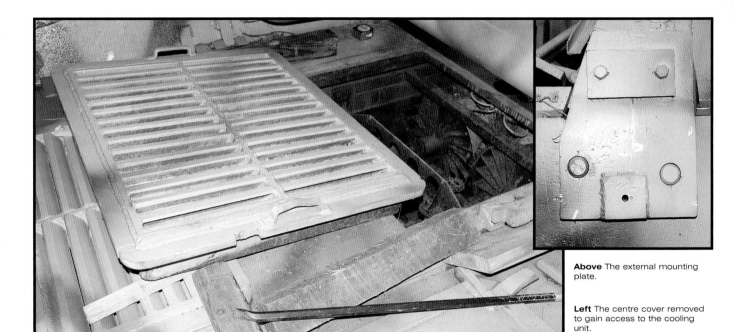

**Above** The external mounting plate.

**Left** The centre cover removed to gain access to the cooling unit.

**Above** Another item found inside the vehicle is the Kettenschließer (Bracket for closing the tracks).

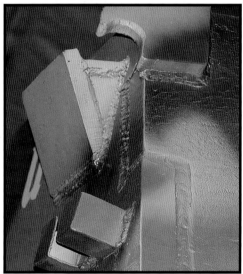

**Above** The armoured cover over the opening for the antenna cable, on top of which the antenna would be mounted.

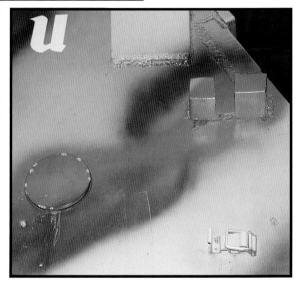

**Above** The brackets for a sledge hammer, the part for the hammer head seemingly modified.

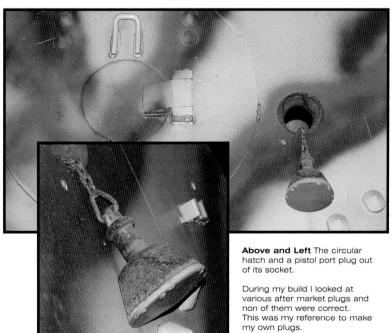

**Above and Left** The circular hatch and a pistol port plug out of its socket.

During my build I looked at various after market plugs and non of them were correct. This was my reference to make my own plugs.

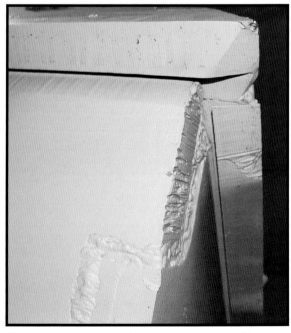

**Above** The recessed lower sides of the superstructure side and rear wall.

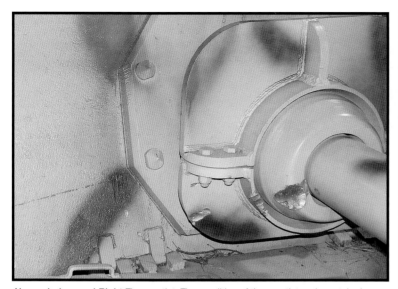

**Above, below and Right** The mantlet. The condition of the mantlet and gun tube is like new, must be the quality of steel used for these parts.

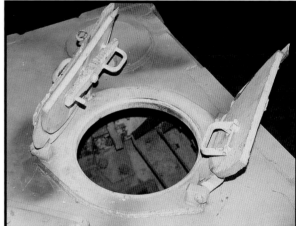

**Above and Below** The loaders hatch.

**Above** The armoured cover for the extractor fan with on each side the supports for the breech hooks.

**Left** top view of the Elefant's commander's cupola. The circular cupola replaced the originally introduced squarish flat commander's hatch. Remnants of the earlier style hatch are visible at the right of the cupola, towards the side wall of the superstructure.

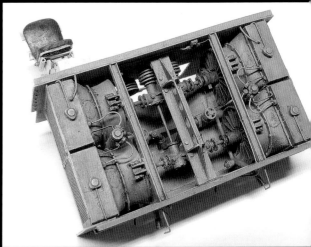

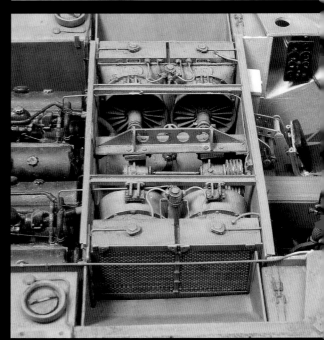

# PAINTING

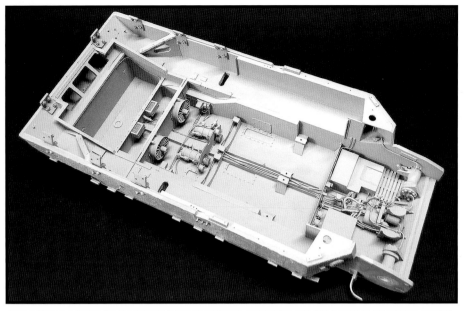
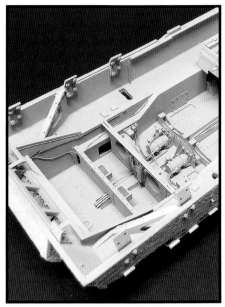

**Above** Before painting the model was taken apart in sub-assemblies and first a coat of primer was applied.

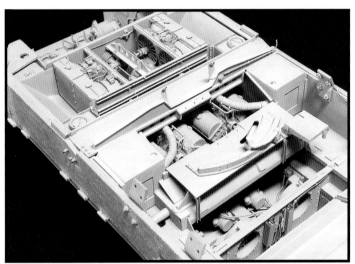
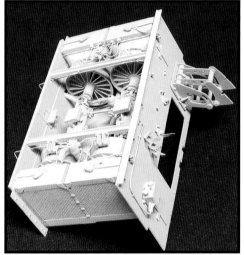

**Above** The fit of all sub assemblies is very tight so after applying a coat of paint I testfitted again to check for fitting issues.

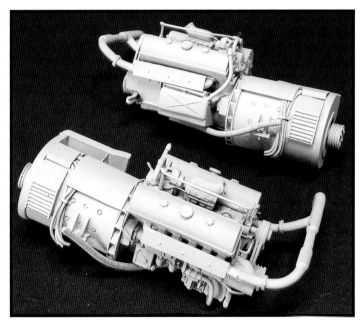
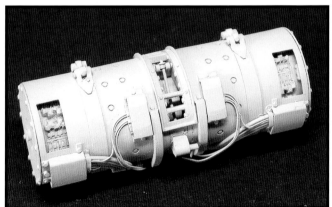
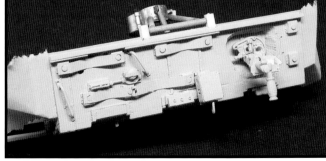

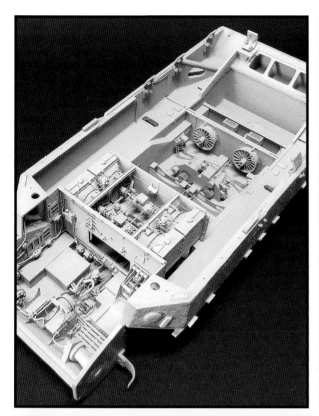

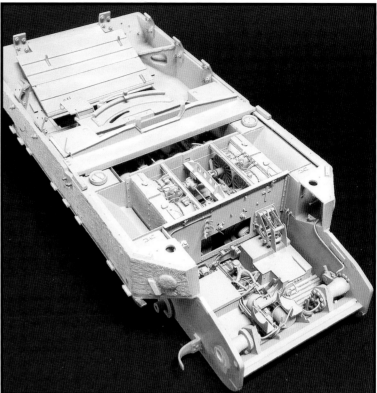

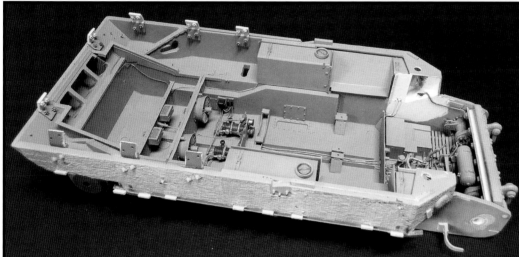

**Left** Colours always are a subject of debate and depend on light, camera, and screen settings. The reference photos show some areas still with paint, mainly Elfenbein and what must have been the Grey-Green colour. Due to the above it was difficult to determine the correct colour even from photos of surviving Panzers with an untouched interior, or even restored Panzers. For the Grey-Green I decided to mix a colour close to and a bit darker than what can be seen in the reference pictures. Still a bit Blue freshly applied, but this changes with weathering.

**Below** For some mechanical components I mixed a colour that some of the real parts still seem to show though it's hard to tell considering the condition of the vehicle and remaining patches of paint.

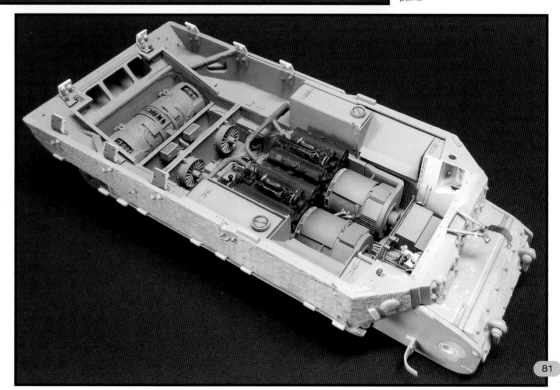

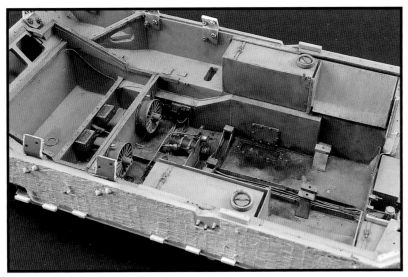

**Above** Before installing the various sub assemblies permanently, detail is hand painted and everything is weathered.

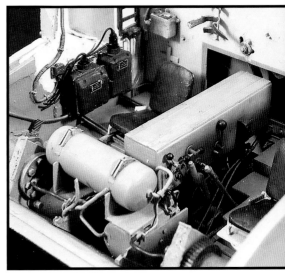

**Above** Seats added and transformers wired, the larger one U10a1 and behind it the EUa2.The driver's seat remains removable to make it possible to remove the cooling unit (radiator/fan assembly) when the frontal armour is fixed in place.

**Left** The drivers instrument panel.

**Above** Note how the Radio Operator's seat is mounted on the battery boxes and the frame secured with butterfly nuts.

| Ammeter | Speed |
|---------|-------|
| Engine rpm | Engine rpm |
| Coolant temp | Panel light switch |
| E-motors temp | Double oil pressure |
| Warning light e-motor overload | Warning light short circuit |

**Above** Throttle connections between floor pedal and engines are made. On the lower firewall between drivers console and control box is a lever for controlling the Anlassvorrichtung (choke) on the carburettors.

**Right** Not a space you want to spend much time in, the RO seat in particular. Imagine the heat produced by the transformers and radio sets and the noise and more heat coming from the engines, generators and fans in the rear. The way the MG-34 is mounted also isn't adding much to the comfort of this workplace.

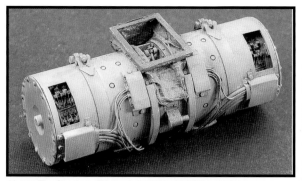

**Above** The Siemens-Shuckert D 1495a 230KW e-motors ready to be installe. On top is the fabric funnel.

**Above** The drive shafts between engines and fans added.

**Above** On the hull floor the engine mounts and the frame with generators.

**Above** The two Maybach HL120 TRM with Siemens-Shuckert K58-8 500VA generators.

**Left** Between the two generators the coolant return hoses. Throttle linkages are attached to the engines and the engine oil pressure lines to the instrument panel are also fitted. In this picture you can see the engine oil pressure lines going up and over the fuel tank, making their way to the driver's/RO's compartment.

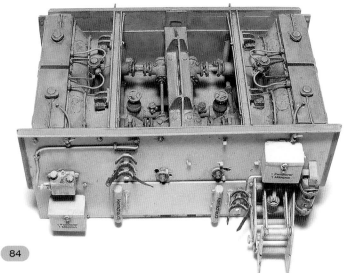

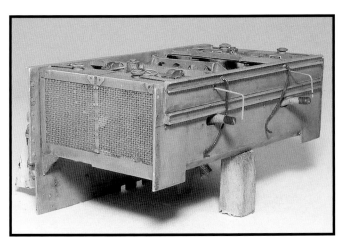

**Above** Only things missing are the drive belts. Since they need to connect with the generators and the cooling unit remains removable they were left off.

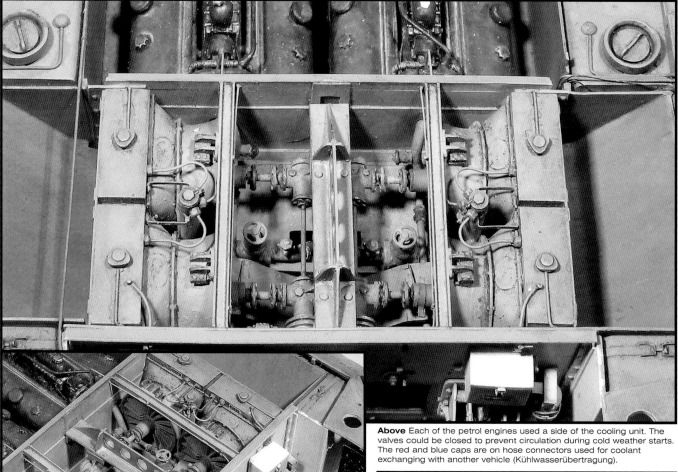

**Above** Each of the petrol engines used a side of the cooling unit. The valves could be closed to prevent circulation during cold weather starts. The red and blue caps are on hose connectors used for coolant exchanging with another vehicle (Kühlwasserübertragung).

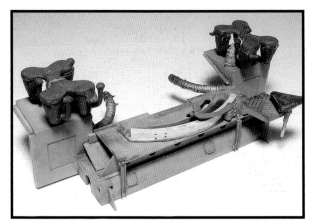

The traverse platform remains removable. The hoses from the air filters fit on the engines intake manifolds.

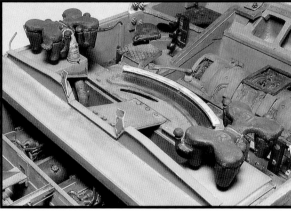

**Above and below** Brücke and Strebe installed, they remain removable.

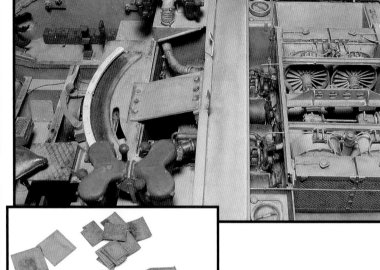

As mentioned earlier there were more ways to store ammo rounds. A few pictures of a driving school Elefant without superstructure shows brackets for three rounds on each sponson. The two forward brackets are of simple design, the front bracket is made from wood and still present in the Ferdinand displayed in Kubinka. The brackets on the rear are not shown in detail in the photos but seem to have had swinging supports for easy loading and unloading rounds and for removing the slanted floor panels.

With the sponson brackets a total of 32 rounds could be stored in fixed positions. The U-shaped profiles on the slanted floor made me wondor if

something could be mounted into them. The profiles align with the two vertical profiles on the traversing platform. Reports mention many more than 32 rounds could be stored
inside and the only available space is on the floor.

Rounds of ammo would fit perfectly between the boards. Note the available floor space for the two loaders. With full ammo racks space was very limited. The boarding is my interpretation of how it could have looked. The idea is that new rounds would be stored in the front section and spent casings in the rear until they could be ejected out of the vehicle.

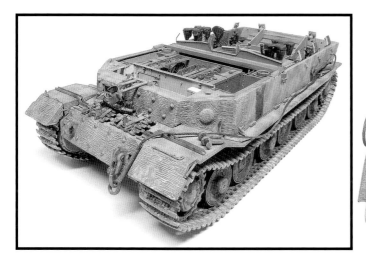

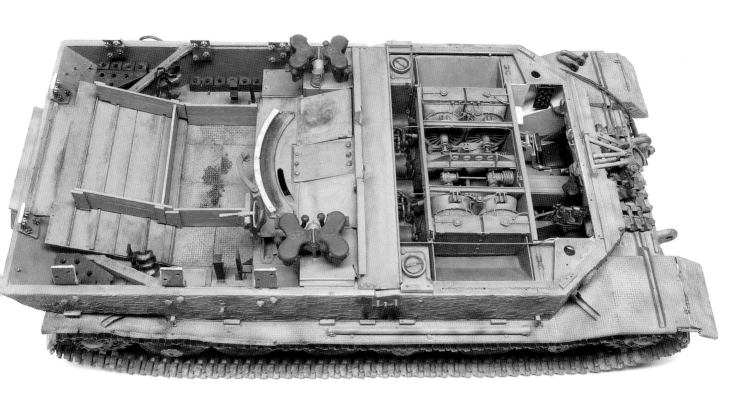

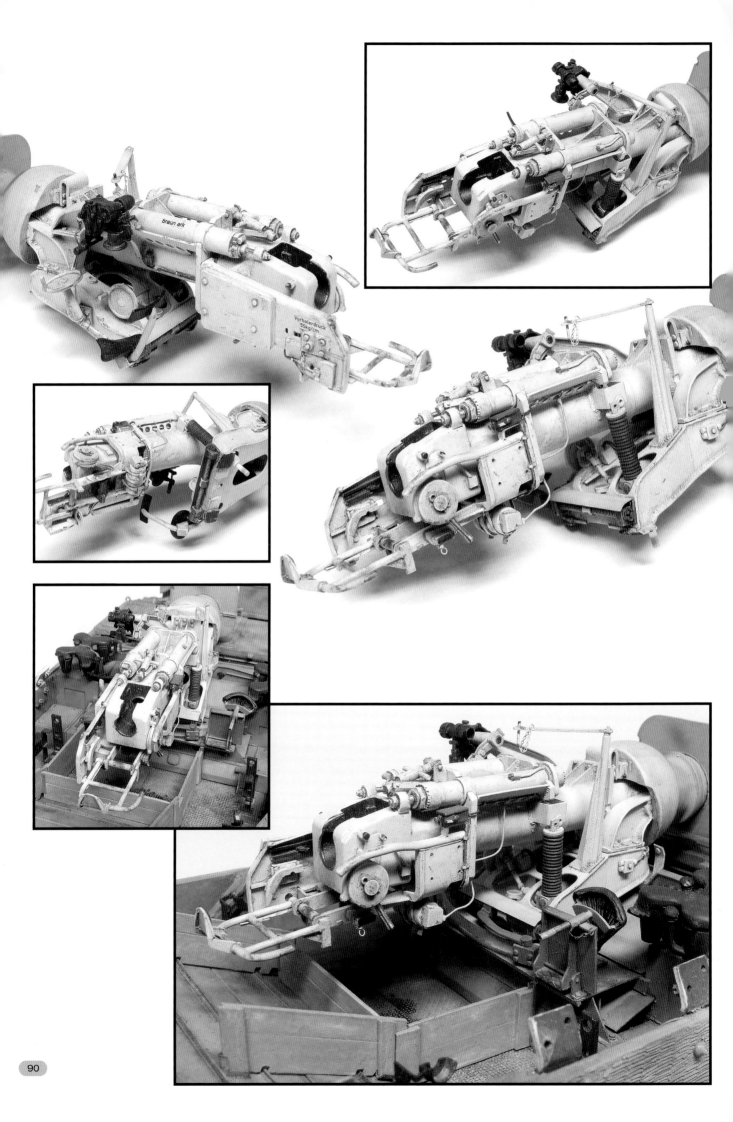

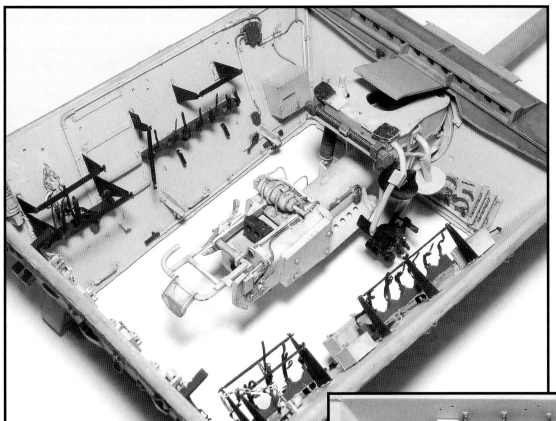

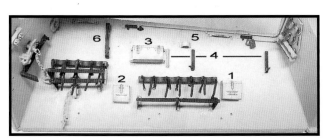

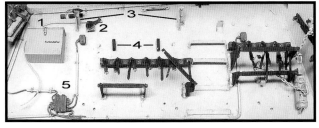

**Above** Superstructure walls detailed and painted. Left side with boxes for the intercom set (1), Nebelkerzen (2) and spare periscopes (3) and brackets for the cleaning rods (4), brush (5) and a bracket for coolant hoses (6)

Right side with a box for Funkzubehor (1), the Maschinentelegraph (2) , brackets for an MG34 (3), MG-34 spare barrel case (4)  and the Kasten Pz. Nr. 6a (5).

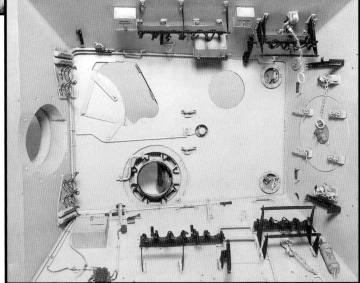

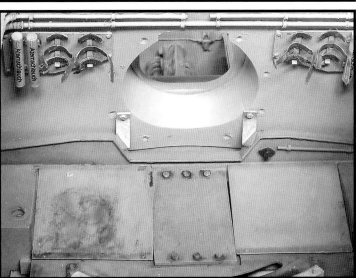

**Above** The opening for the main gun showing again how thick the frontal armour is. Also note the pipes for the electric wiring, all bends are made from flexible metal tubing. The two vertical strips on the Brücke and bolted against the frontal armour support the main gun when the superstructure was removed from the hull.

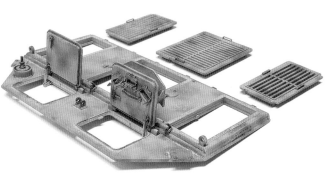

**Below** With full ammo racks space for the two loaders would be very limited and if the space between the wooden dividers was used for extra rounds it even would be less. Then imagine the gun traversing!

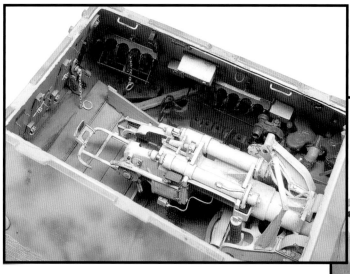

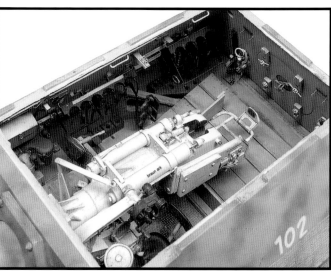

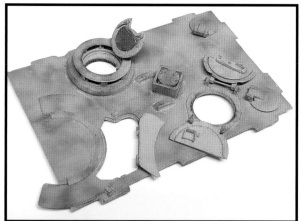

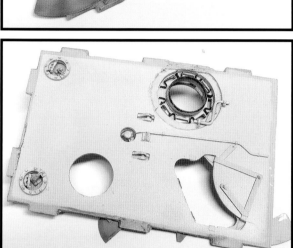

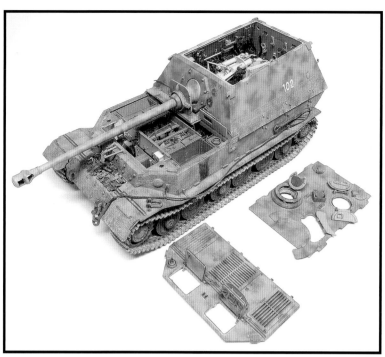

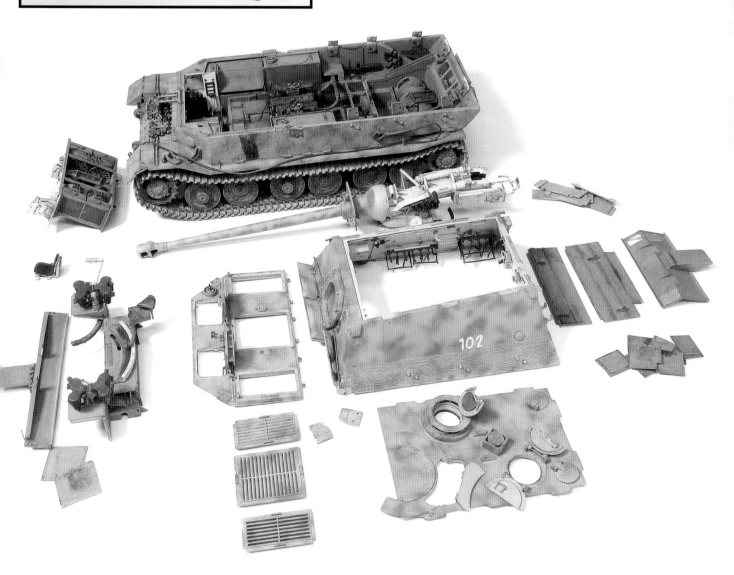

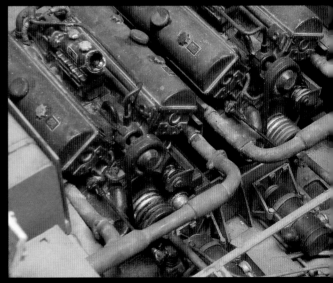

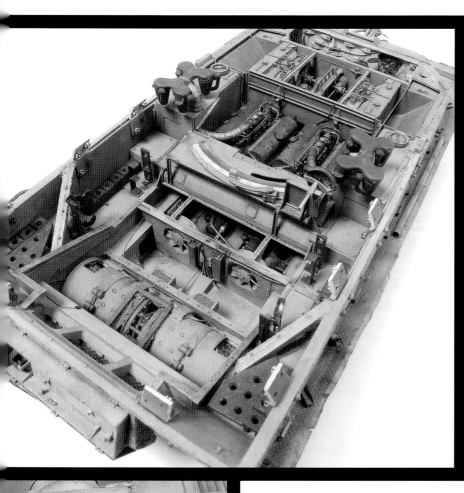

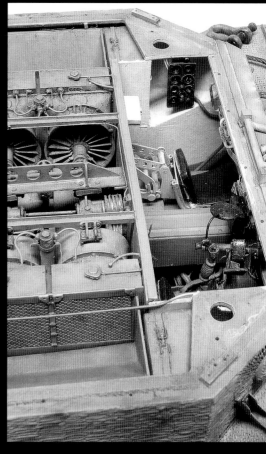

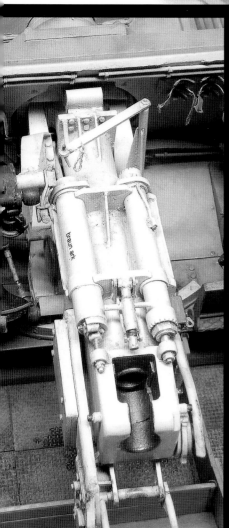

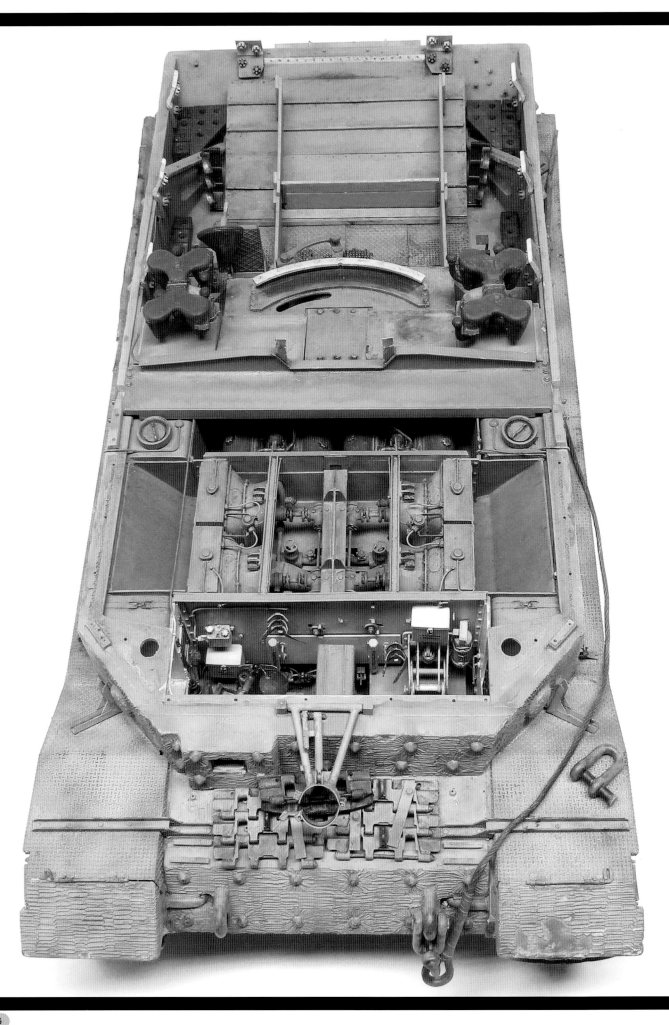

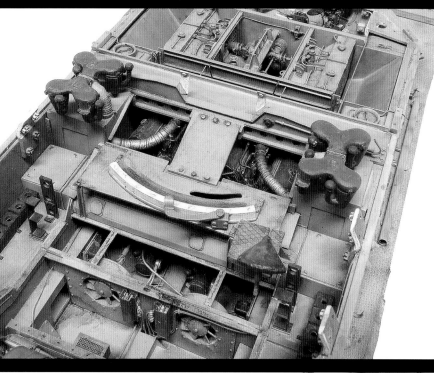

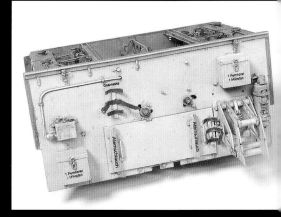

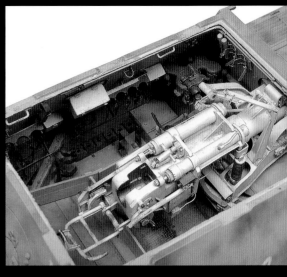

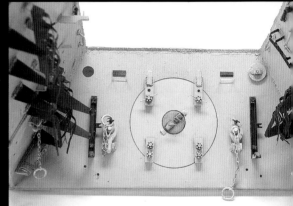

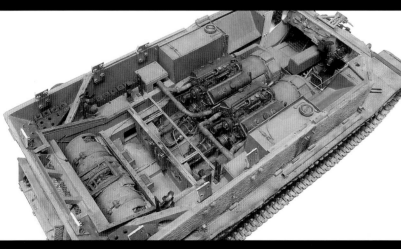